LANGUAGE ARTS

WEEKLY

PRACTICE

Grade 1

Credits
Author: Jennifer B. Stith
Copy Editor: Elise Craver

Visit *carsondellosa.com* for correlations to Common Core, state, national, and Canadian provincial standards.

Carson-Dellosa Publishing, LLC
PO Box 35665
Greensboro, NC 27425 USA
carsondellosa.com

978-1-4838-2789-6
01-053167784

Table of Contents

Introduction

The Weekly Practice series provides 40 weeks of essential daily practice in either math or language arts. It is the perfect supplement to any classroom curriculum and provides standards-based activities for every day of the week but Friday.

The activities are intended as homework assignments for Monday through Thursday and cover a wide spectrum of standards-based skills. The skills are presented at random to provide comprehensive learning but are repeated systematically throughout the book. The intention is to offer regular, focused practice to ensure mastery and retention.

Each 192-page book provides 40 weeks of reproducible pages, a standards alignment matrix, flash cards, and an answer key. The reproducible pages are perfect for homework but also work well for morning work, early finishers, and warm-up activities.

About This Book

Each page contains a variety of short, fun exercises that build in difficulty across the span of the book. The activities are divided into two sections:

- The Daily Extension Activities at the front of the book are intended to engage both student and family. These off-the-page activities are simple and fun so that students will look forward to this practice time at home. The activities span one week at a time. The instructions are clear and simple so that students can follow them with or without assistance in their homes. None need be returned to school.

- The daily practice section involves more comprehensive learning. Because of the simplicity of directions and straightforward tasks, students will be able to complete most tasks independently in a short period of time. There are four pages of activities per week, allowing for testing or a student break on Friday if desired. These pages are intended to be brought back to school.

Pages can be offered in any order, making it possible to reinforce specific skills when needed. However, skills are repeated regularly throughout the book to ensure retention over time, making a strong case for using pages sequentially.

An answer key is included for the daily practice section. You can check answers as a group for a quick follow-up lesson or monitor students' progress individually. Follow the basic page layout provided at the beginning of the answer key to match answers to page placement. Also included in the book is a set of flash cards. Reproduce them to give to students for at-home practice, or place them in classroom centers.

Common Core State Standards
Alignment Matrix

Standard	W1	W2	W3	W4	W5	W6	W7	W8	W9	W10	W11	W12	W13	W14	W15	W16	W17	W18	W19	W20
I.RL.1	●		●		●		●		●		●		●		●		●		●	
I.RL.2																				
I.RL.3	●		●		●		●		●		●		●		●		●		●	
I.RL.4																				
I.RL.5																				
I.RL.6																				
I.RL.7	●		●		●		●		●		●		●		●		●		●	
I.RL.9																				
I.RL.10	●		●		●		●		●			●	●		●	●	●		●	
I.RI.1				●																●
I.RI.2		●																		
I.RI.3				●																
I.RI.4																				
I.RI.5		●		●		●		●		●				●		●		●		●
I.RI.6		●		●		●		●		●		●		●		●		●		●
I.RI.7																				
I.RI.8		●		●		●		●		●		●		●		●		●		●
I.RI.9																				
I.RI.10		●		●		●		●		●		●		●		●		●		●
I.RF.1	●	●	●	●	●	●	●	●	●	●	●	●	●	●	●	●	●	●	●	●
I.RF.2	●	●	●	●	●	●	●	●	●	●	●	●	●	●	●	●	●	●	●	●
I.RF.3	●	●	●	●	●	●	●	●	●	●	●	●	●	●	●	●	●	●	●	●
I.RF.4	●	●	●	●	●	●	●	●	●	●	●	●	●	●	●	●	●	●	●	●
I.W.1		●				●					●			●		●		●		
I.W.2		●							●											
I.W.3			●		●															
I.W.5		●		●		●		●			●			●		●		●		●
I.W.6																				
I.W.7												●		●		●		●		●
I.W.8																				
I.L.1	●	●	●	●	●	●	●	●	●	●	●	●	●	●	●	●	●	●	●	●
I.L.2	●	●	●	●	●	●	●	●	●	●	●	●	●	●	●	●	●	●	●	●
I.L.4																				
I.L.5	●	●	●	●	●	●	●	●	●	●	●	●	●	●	●	●	●	●	●	●
I.L.6																					

W = Week

Common Core State Standards
Alignment Matrix

Standard	W21	W22	W23	W24	W25	W26	W27	W28	W29	W30	W31	W32	W33	W34	W35	W36	W37	W38	W39	W40
1.RL.1	●		●		●		●		●		●		●		●		●		●	
1.RL.2																				
1.RL.3	●		●		●				●	●	●	●		●	●		●		●	
1.RL.4	●			●					●		●				●					
1.RL.5																				
1.RL.6																				
1.RL.7	●		●		●		●		●		●		●		●		●		●	
1.RL.9														●	●	●		●		
1.RL.10	●		●		●		●		●		●		●		●		●		●	
1.RI.1				●								●						●		
1.RI.2												●						●		●
1.RI.3												●								
1.RI.4				●														●		
1.RI.5				●		●			●	●		●		●		●	●	●		
1.RI.6		●		●		●		●			●		●		●		●	●		●
1.RI.7																		●		
1.RI.8		●		●		●		●			●		●		●			●		●
1.RI.9																				
1.RI.10		●		●		●		●			●		●		●		●			●
1.RF.1	●	●	●	●	●	●	●	●	●	●	●	●	●	●	●	●	●	●	●	●
1.RF.2	●	●	●	●	●	●	●	●	●	●	●	●	●	●	●	●	●	●	●	●
1.RF.3	●	●	●	●	●	●	●	●	●	●	●	●	●	●	●	●	●	●	●	●
1.RF.4	●	●	●	●	●	●	●	●	●	●	●	●	●	●	●	●	●	●	●	●
1.W.1					●		●		●		●		●		●		●		●	
1.W.2			●							●										
1.W.3	●																			
1.W.5		●		●		●		●			●		●		●		●		●	
1.W.6																				
1.W.7																				
1.W.8																				
1.L.1	●	●	●	●	●	●	●	●	●	●	●	●	●	●	●	●	●	●	●	●
1.L.2	●	●	●	●	●	●	●	●	●	●	●	●	●	●	●	●	●	●	●	●
1.L.4				●								●						●	●	●
1.L.5	●	●	●	●	●	●	●	●	●	●	●	●	●	●	●	●	●	●	●	●
1.L.6																				

W = Week

School to Home Communication

The research is clear that family involvement is strongly linked to student success. Support for student learning at home improves student achievement in school. Educators should not underestimate the significance of this connection.

The activities in this book create an opportunity to create or improve this school-to-home link. The activities span a week at a time and can be sent home as a week-long homework packet each Monday. Simply clip together the strip of fun activities from the front of the book with the pages for Days 1 to 4 for the correct week.

Most of the activities can be completed independently, but many encourage feedback or interaction with a family member. The activities are simple and fun, aiming to create a brief pocket of learning that is enjoyable to all.

In order to make the school-to-home program work for students and their families, we encourage you to reach out to them with an introductory letter. Explain the program and its intent and ask them to partner with you in their children's educational process. Describe the role you expect them to play. Encourage them to offer suggestions or feedback along the way.

A sample letter is included below. Use it as is or create your own letter to introduce this project and elicit their collaboration.

Dear Families,

I anticipate a productive and exciting year of learning and look forward to working with you and your child. We have a lot of work to do! I hope we—teacher, student, and family—can work together as a team to achieve the goal of academic progress we all hope for this year.

I will send home a packet of homework each week on _____. There will be two items to complete each day: a single task on a strip plus a full page of focused practice. Each page or strip is labeled Day 1 (for Monday), Day 2, Day 3, or Day 4. There is no homework on Friday.

Please make sure that your student brings back the completed work _____. It is important that these are brought in on time as we may work on some of the lessons as a class.

If you have any questions about this program or would like to talk to me about it, please feel free to call or email me. Thank you for joining me in making this the best year ever for your student!

Sincerely,

_____
Name

_____
Phone

_____
Email

	Day 1	Day 2	Day 3	Day 4
Week 1	Recite a favorite nursery rhyme. Act out the poem, using props if desired.	Use sidewalk chalk to write letters on an outside surface. Have a friend say a word. Hop from letter to letter as you spell the word aloud.	Write a sight word on an index card. Cut apart the letters of the word. Have an adult flip over one letter and see if you can guess which letter(s) are missing.	Write at least five, three-letter object words on self-stick notes. Stick the notes to the objects in your home. For example, put *pot* on a kitchen sauce pot or teapot.

	Day 1	Day 2	Day 3	Day 4
Week 2	Gather some kitchen tools and repair tools. Place them in a pile. Sort the tools by their purpose or category.	Make a set of letter tiles on squares of paper. Choose four letter tiles that make one word. Mix them up and rearrange the letters to make the word.	Write the letters of the alphabet next to the numbers on a dot-to-dot puzzle. Connect the letters in ABC order. Then, white out the numbers.	Fill a cookie sheet with salt. Write letters on index cards. Choose a letter. Trace the letter in the salt. Gently shake the pan to erase the letter and repeat for other letters.

	Day 1	Day 2	Day 3	Day 4
Week 3	Write a set of upper- and lowercase letters on index cards. Deal five cards to each player and put the remaining cards in the center. Play Go Fish by taking turns and matching pairs of the same letter.	Choose a page from a book that has many rhymes. Put plastic wrap over the page. Use a write-on/wipe-away marker to circle the rhyming words.	Cut out pictures of objects in magazines and label them *singular* or *plural*. For example, cut out a picture of one apple. Then, cut out a picture of two apples. Label each picture with the correct word.	Write words on index cards that make a silly sentence when put together. For example, *The baby jumped over the monkey*. Rearrange the words to make the silly sentence.

	Day 1	Day 2	Day 3	Day 4
Week 4	Cut out food pictures from grocery store ads and magazines. Sort the food pictures by color. Glue the pictures to a piece of construction paper that is the same color.	Play tic-tac-toe with words. Make a large grid on a piece of paper. Each person chooses a word family such as *-ad* and *-ap* and takes a turn writing words from her word family on the grid.	Write words from different categories on index cards. Lay out four cards. Three cards should have words from the same category. Tell which word does not belong and explain why.	Have an adult say a spelling word aloud. Write the first letter on a piece of paper. Then, write the first two letters on the next row. Continue until the word is complete and the result looks like a staircase.

	Day 1	Day 2	Day 3	Day 4
Week 5	Write upper- and lowercase letters on cards. Play a game of Memory by matching the uppercase and lowercase letters of the alphabet.	Take a verb, such as *hop,* and practice using time words so that you hear the differences in tense. *Yesterday, I hopped. Today, I hop. Tomorrow, I will hop.* Repeat with other verbs.	On index cards, write several nouns that add *-s* in their plural forms. Write *s* on another card. Read each noun in its singular form. Then, place the *s* at the end and say the plural form.	On an index card, write the word *dad.* Cut more index cards in thirds and write *b, f, h, l, m, p,* or *t* on each piece. Place a letter on top of the first *d* in *dad.* Say the new word. Repeat with each letter.
Week 6	Have an adult collect some items from around your home. Return each item to its proper place and explain why it goes there, using the item's category and purpose.	Find an article or advertisement in a magazine or newspaper. Use a marker to circle any uppercase or lowercase letter *Ffs* that you find.	Look at the picture on a book page and tell a family member what is happening, where the story takes place, who is doing something, etc. Then, read the words and talk about how they relate.	Share something about your day with a family member. Keep adding more details. Then, work together to summarize the report in one strong sentence.
Week 7	Choose an animal that has something to offer people, such as the black sheep in "Baa, Baa, Black Sheep." Use the same rhythm from that nursery rhyme to create an original rhyme with a friend.	Have an adult write the upper- and lowercase forms of a letter on a self-stick note and the letters in dotted lines on another. Trace the letters on both notes. Then, write them on a piece of paper.	Make a T-chart with the headings *Inside* and *Outside.* Complete the chart with things that are inside or outside your home. Have a friend do the same. The person with the most original words wins.	Find an object in the room and tell a family member clues that describe the object. Be specific! For example, instead of telling where, tell where it is in relation to another object.
Week 8	Find and cut out charts from catalogs and magazines. Discuss the purpose of the charts to a reader. Talk about how to read the charts.	Play tic-tac-toe with words. Make a large grid on a piece of paper. Each person chooses a word family such as *-ed* and *-en* and takes a turn writing words from his word family on the grid.	Read a nonfiction and a fiction book on the same topic. Discuss what information you learn about the topic from each type of text. How are they the same and different?	Spell words one letter at a time with another person. The first person says a word such as *bird.* The second person says the first letter. Take turns spelling the word by adding one letter at a time.

	Day 1	Day 2	Day 3	Day 4
Week 9	Have an adult hide lowercase letters written on cards. Give the seeker the uppercase letters and have her choose a letter to find the lowercase version of. The adult should give clues as needed.	Find a stick. Then, find a dirt patch in your yard or neighborhood. Have a friend or family member say a letter and use the stick to practice writing the letter.	Write the letters of a word on an index card. Cut the index card apart between the letters and then mix up the letters. Remove one letter. Make the word again and say the letter that is missing.	Read a story with an adult. Have the adult ask questions about the story. Answer the questions and point out the places in the book where you found the information to support your answers.

	Day 1	Day 2	Day 3	Day 4
Week 10	Check out books with titles that are opposites from the library. Explain what makes the words opposites. See if you can come up with other opposite word pairs.	Make a cluster map about your favorite topic. Write the topic in a center bubble. Then, use books or other resources to learn and write facts around the outside. Connect related ideas with lines.	Choose three related toys and one unrelated toy. Place them in a line and have someone figure out which one doesn't belong. Have them explain the reason for their choice.	Write a spelling word on a sheet of paper. Place tracing paper or white tissue paper over the word. Trace it with a pencil or crayon. Move the paper and trace the word again in a different color.

	Day 1	Day 2	Day 3	Day 4
Week 11	Before reading a book, look through the pictures and tell a family member what you can learn about characters and settings from just the pictures.	Use a daily journal. Write a note about your day and leave the journal for a family member to read. Write back and forth, asking questions and adding details each day.	Use conjunctions when you discuss the weather each day. For example, say, "Yesterday was hot, but today is going to be hotter." Or, "It is supposed to rain today, but it will be sunny tomorrow."	On an index card, write the word *bat*. Cut index cards in thirds and write *e*, *i*, *o*, or *u* on each piece. Place a vowel on top of the *a* in *bat*. Say the new word. Repeat with each letter.

	Day 1	Day 2	Day 3	Day 4
Week 12	Ask family members to help you practice spelling words. Assign each person a letter of a spelling word. On your mark, everyone must try to form, or unscramble, the word.	Choose one thing that you do each day, such as packing your backpack. On an index card, write the steps, in order, for how you do it. Give the card to a friend and see if they can follow your steps.	Print pictures of objects whose names have the *ar*, *er*, *ir*, *or*, and *ur* spelling patterns. Say each picture's name aloud and sort the words by their vowel sounds.	Write the names of your family members and their positions or roles in the family (baby, sister, etc.) on index cards. Sort the cards into a proper noun and a common noun pile.

	Day 1	Day 2	Day 3	Day 4
Week 13	Have an adult write a grocery list for the week. Then, rewrite the list in ABC order.	Use chenille stems or yarn to form an uppercase and lowercase letter M. Can you make any other letters?	Act out a word to figure out whether it is a noun or a verb. For example, can you get up and then *sit*? Yes! Can you get up and then *spider*? No!	Look at announcements for upcoming events in newspapers or magazines. Circle the proper nouns. Look for names, places, and dates.

	Day 1	Day 2	Day 3	Day 4
Week 14	Look through a favorite picture book and find words that have two syllables. Write any of the words that have a double consonant where you would divide the word into its syllables.	Use small labels to relabel a die with word families such as -in, -ip, -ig, -it, -id, and -ib. Roll the die and write as many words as you can think of for that word family.	Write sight words on index cards. On the backs, draw the word's shape using tall and short boxes. For example, *the* would be tall box, tall box, short box. Use each word shape to figure out the sight word.	With an adult, fill six wells of an ice cube tray with water. Drop three to five drops of food coloring in each well. Then, use a paintbrush to paint sight words onto a piece of white toast.

	Day 1	Day 2	Day 3	Day 4
Week 15	Use your senses to make a list of adjectives that describe an apple or other piece of fruit. Try to use all five senses.	Create an advertisement for your favorite toy. Use adjectives to describe your toy. Persuade others to make the toy a favorite too.	Write 15 singular words and 15 plural words on index cards. Place them all facedown. Flip over two cards. If they are both singular or both plural, keep them. If not, flip them back over.	Find a simple sentence from a book you have read. Write each word on an index card. Mix up the cards and try to recreate the sentence. Check the book to see if you are correct.

	Day 1	Day 2	Day 3	Day 4
Week 16	Make an opposites word dictionary. Write a pair of opposites at the top of each page. Draw a picture for each word. Make sure the pictures show how the words have opposite meanings.	Use a set of magnetic letters to make words. Place letters that spell a specific word onto a cookie sheet. Then, rearrange the letters to make other two-, three-, and four-letter words.	Use three counters or chips to stretch the sounds in three-letter words. Line up the counters. As you say each sound in the word, move one counter forward.	Write each word of a simple sentence on an index card. Write additional words that can be added between the other words to make the sentence longer.

	Day 1	Day 2	Day 3	Day 4
Week 17	Look at a scene in a book. Make a list of all of the things you see. Rewrite the list in ABC order.	Write three-letter words on index cards. Write the consonants in black and the vowels in the middles of the words in red. Sort the words by their vowels.	Copy sentences from a story or article. Use markers to circle the nouns in one color and the pronouns in another color.	Choose a sight word to be the word of the day. Keep a tally of every time you see the word in books, on signs, etc.

	Day 1	Day 2	Day 3	Day 4
Week 18	Write two-syllable words on index cards. Use scissors to cut each word apart between the syllables. Compare the words and discuss how the words are divided.	Cut out a large uppercase letter *R* from construction paper. Write words beginning with *R* on the uppercase *R*. Be sure to include both common and proper nouns.	Gather pictures of objects whose names have the /oy/, /ow/, and /aw/ vowel sounds. Say the name of each object. Use a mirror to watch how your mouth forms the different vowel sounds.	Pretend you have received a postcard from a traveling friend. Write the postcard and draw a picture. Include the place he or she visited. Be sure to use capital letters for each proper noun.

	Day 1	Day 2	Day 3	Day 4
Week 19	Write at least 10 adjectives on index cards. Place them facedown in a pile. Turn one card over. Read the adjective and tell a noun that it describes (for example, heavy rock).	Use cooked and cooled spaghetti noodles to practice the letter *s*. Form a letter *s* on construction paper. Let the noodle dry. Trace your finger along the letter *s*.	Write the same sight word on four index cards. Choose one. Cover one letter on each card with a self-stick note. Try to figure out the hidden letter. Lift the note to check your answer. Repeat.	Write a simple sentence on a sheet of paper. Rewrite the sentence, but change one of the words. Repeat until your final sentence no longer contains any of the original sentence´s words.

	Day 1	Day 2	Day 3	Day 4
Week 20	Read a list of at least eight two-syllable words. Write each word on an index card. Cut the cards in half between the syllables and match the correct halves to recreate the words.	Draw a 4 × 4 grid. Choose two words and write each word in the grid with one letter in each square. Fill in the rest of the squares with random letters. Challenge a friend to find the words you hid.	Write three sentences from a nonfiction book on strips. Add one sentence that does not belong. Challenge a friend to arrange the strips so that the text makes sense and the extra sentence is removed.	Use chalk to write letters that spell a word down a set of outside stairs. Write the first letter on the top step. Write the first and second letters on the next step. Continue until the word is complete.

	Day 1	Day 2	Day 3	Day 4
Week 21	Make a paper bag puppet for your favorite fairy tale character. Include details that help others know who it is. Use your puppet to act out a part of the fairy tale.	Write a sentence with the verb missing. Write the past, present, and future form of the verb on self-stick notes. Place each verb tense on the missing space and tell how the sentence changes.	Choose your favorite animal. Draw a chart with the headings *Adjectives* and *Verbs.* List at least three adjectives that describe the animal and three verbs that tell what the animal does.	Find four sentences that contain common nouns. Rewrite each sentence, changing the common nouns to proper nouns.
Week 22	Write the letters of a spelling word on bottle caps. Place the caps, or "eggs," inside an empty egg carton. Shake it. Open the carton and "unscramble" the eggs to spell the word.	Write letters on paper scraps. Include at least 10 V's. Scatter the papers in a room. Use a handheld vacuum cleaner to vacuum (or pick up by hand) only the scraps with V's.	Write 10 sight words on index cards. Use different color crayons to draw boxes around each letter of each word.	Use chalk to write a spelling word up a set of outside stairs. Write the full word on the bottom step. Write the word minus the last letter on the next step. Continue until only the first letter remains.
Week 23	Make a list of words that end in *-ing*. Circle the verbs. Underline the simple verb within each word (for example, underline *jump* in *jumping*).	Use gummy worms to form the letter *W*. Use four worms to make each line of the *W*. Can you make any other letters?	Choose a pair of homophones (for example, *hair* and *hare*). Draw a picture showing each word, such as a hare with long hair. Label each part of the picture with the correct word.	Write a brochure about your town. Fold a sheet of paper in thirds. On the front, draw a picture and write the town's name. On the inside, write proper nouns that you would find in your town.
Week 24	Create a crossword puzzle using four short *i* words. Connect all four words by at least one letter in each word. For example, *dish* and *lips* could connect at their *i*´s or *s*´s.	Cut out adjectives from the headlines and advertisements in a newspaper. Glue them on a sheet of paper.	Find a picture of a flower online or in a book or magazine. Tell what words in the text match the image you see on the screen or in print.	Place a thin layer of baking soda on a cookie sheet. Practice writing your sight words or spelling words for the week in the baking soda.

	Day 1	Day 2	Day 3	Day 4
Week 25	Choose a poem that has verbs in all the same tense. Recite the poem changing the tense of each verb. You may have to change the form of other words in the poem as well.	Use chalk to write the alphabet in two columns on a sidewalk. Stand with two feet at the beginnings of the columns. Use one foot to hop to each letter to spell a word as it is read to you.	Write the word *like* at the top of a sheet of paper. Make a list of all of the new words you can think of by adding a prefix, suffix, or both to the word.	Find an article or advertisement in a magazine or newspaper. Use a marker to circle any uppercase or lowercase letter *Nn's* that you find.

	Day 1	Day 2	Day 3	Day 4
Week 26	Think of something that is simple for you to make. Write directions for how to make it. See if a family member can follow your directions.	Think of a story about a lonely frog. Tell the beginning, middle, and end of the story to a family member.	Place some items of clothing in a pile. Select three that are worn in winter. Select one that is worn in summer. Place them in front of a friend and challenge them to tell which does not belong and why.	Pretend a smelly sock is hidden in your room. Tell a friend five places to look for the sock using a preposition in each instruction. For example, "Look beside the soccer ball on the floor."

	Day 1	Day 2	Day 3	Day 4
Week 27	Find pictures of your family members' favorite things. Cut out the pictures and add a caption for each one, using a possessive noun (for example, *Dave's guitar*).	Create picture cards for words that have the /ch/ sound. Say the name of each picture and tell where the /ch/ sound is found in the word.	Make a list of long *i* words. Underline the different spellings of the vowel sound in different colors.	Create a word search puzzle on a sheet of graph paper. Choose three words and write each one three times. Fill in the remaining squares with random letters. Challenge a friend to find all of your words.

	Day 1	Day 2	Day 3	Day 4
Week 28	Write a tongue twister sentence using mostly words that have the digraph *th*. For example, *The three-toed sloth thought that the thorns were teeth.*	Write a sequence of letters that contain a secret word (for example, *e s b a l l o g*). Have a friend find the word by giving her a clue to the meaning of the word.	A dictionary lists words in ABC order. Find two other resources that use ABC order to organize their information.	Pretend you just got a gift card for music downloads. Make a list of three song titles or albums you would like to download. Use correct capitalization.

	Day 1	Day 2	Day 3	Day 4
Week 29	Compare a page in a dictionary to a page of a glossary. Tell the similarities and differences.	Write a letter to your family members telling why your current bedtime should be changed.	Write a sentence using each word in one of the following pairs: *dad, Dad; mom, Mom; grandma, Grandma;* and *grandpa, Grandpa.*	Write a sentence on a strip of paper using words that can also be rearranged to make an entirely new sentence. Cut apart the words and try to make different sentences.

	Day 1	Day 2	Day 3	Day 4
Week 30	Write a short story about a water droplet. Give it a name and tell about its travels through the water cycle. Use the correct vocabulary to describe what happens to the water droplet.	Choose a handful of letter tiles or magnetic letters. See how many two-letter words you can make. Then, try to make three-letter words. Finally, find the longest word you can make from the letters.	Draw and label a diagram of an octopus. Use the Internet or other resources to find out information about octopuses and to help you label your diagram.	Look through a catalog or magazine. Find and cut out a picture whose caption might ask a question, tell a statement, or exclaim something. Write the caption under the picture.

	Day 1	Day 2	Day 3	Day 4
Week 31	Find an article or advertisement in a magazine or newspaper. Use a marker to circle any uppercase or lowercase letter *Aa's* that you find.	Think of a word that begins with a /ch/ sound, a word that ends with a /ch/ sound, and a word that contains a /ch/ sound in the middle of the word.	Think of all of the different ways you can tell someone, "Good job!" Change the word *good* to other words. Tell three people today that they are doing a good job, but use the new words instead.	Look at a map of the United States. Point to the capital letter(s) in each state's name.

	Day 1	Day 2	Day 3	Day 4
Week 32	Act out something that is easy for you to do. Act out something that is difficult for you to do.	Copy a story. Circle in yellow all of the past tense verbs. Underline any words in the sentence that serve as clues to the tense of the verbs such as *yesterday, last week,* etc.	Write a sentence using all of the following words: *give, once,* and *thank.*	Who is your favorite storybook character? Write a list of traits the character has and draw a picture.

	Day 1	Day 2	Day 3	Day 4
Week 33	Draw a poster explaining why washing your hands is important. Use bold words, diagrams, pictures, and facts.	The long e sound can be spelled in many different ways. Find and write all of the ways a long e can be spelled. Write the entire word.	*It's* and *its* are words that are homophones. Think of two other contractions that have homophones. Write each word and the word it sounds like.	Create a word ladder starting with the word *cub* and ending with the word *rag*. Change one letter of the word on each "rung" of the ladder until you reach the final word.
Week 34	Cut apart an apple. Locate the different parts. Draw a diagram of the inside of the apple. Label the diagram with the correct parts of the apple.	Find out how adding the prefix *un-* to a word changes its meaning. Find words in a newspaper article that have the prefix *un-*. Write the meaning of each word.	Make a set of verb cards. Place the cards in one pile if you do the action with your entire body. Place the cards in another pile if you only use one part of your body.	Fill a resealable plastic bag with paint or glue. Squeeze the air out and seal the bag. Place the bag on a flat surface. Use magnetic letters and gently press each letter onto the bag to spell a word.
Week 35	Copy a story or article. Circle words that together make a contraction (for example, *you will*). Write the contraction above each word pair circled.	Fold a sheet of paper in half lengthwise. Write a list of spelling words down the left side. Then, write a scrambled version of each word on the right side. Challenge a friend to draw lines connecting each pair.	Write a set of eight singular words and their irregular plural forms on sixteen cards. Place them facedown in a grid. Play Memory with the cards, collecting singular and plural pairs.	Write a sentence from a favorite story. Change each noun, verb, and adjective. Read the new sentence aloud. Tell how it changes the story.
Week 36	Cut out a letter *E* from construction paper. Write 10 words that make the long e sound on one side of the letter. Flip it over. Write 10 words that make the short e sound on the other side.	Use small labels or stickers to cover the faces of a die with six different letters. Roll the die and write the letter. Repeat five times. Use the letters to make words.	Create a glossary page for a book about ice cream. Include at least four words.	Create your own restaurant menu. Fold a sheet of paper in half width-wise. On the front of the menu, write the restaurant name and your name. On the inside of the menu, list the items you will serve.

	Day 1	Day 2	Day 3	Day 4
Week 37	Tell a friend something you did yesterday, are doing today, and will do tomorrow. Can you use the same verb for all three things? Why or why not?	Try adding a silent *e* to the end of some three-letter words. Can you turn any of the words into words that have long vowel sounds?	Write a sight word on an index card. Cut apart the letters and put them in an envelope. Remove all but one letter from the envelope. Use the remaining letters to spell the word. Tell the missing letter.	Cut out a large question mark from construction paper. Write words on the question mark that often begin question sentences, such as *why* and *what*.

	Day 1	Day 2	Day 3	Day 4
Week 38	Draw a picture of a *simple* house. Then, draw a picture of a *fancy* palace. Tell how the two adjectives are different.	Choose a page in a book you are reading. Place a piece of plastic wrap over the page. Use a write-on/wipe-away marker to find and circle words that have prefixes or suffixes.	Draw a beach scene. Label the nouns in your picture. Share your picture with a family member.	Write a simple sentence about a community helper. Think: *What does he look like? What tools does he use?* Use the answers to add descriptive words to your sentence to make it stronger.

	Day 1	Day 2	Day 3	Day 4
Week 39	Fold a sheet of construction paper in half lengthwise. Cut the top fold into four flaps. Write *First, Next, Then,* and *Finally* on the tops of the flaps. Under each flap, write the stages of a frog's life cycle.	Write a letter to your family convincing them that you want to move to a different country. Tell where and give at least three reasons explaining why you want to move there.	Write three sentences using the words *could, would,* and *should.* Use different ending punctuation marks for each sentence.	Create a word ladder starting with the word *king* and ending with the word *pink.* Change one letter of the word at each "rung" of the ladder.

	Day 1	Day 2	Day 3	Day 4
Week 40	Find a recipe. Draw an illustrated instruction for each step. Share your illustration with a family member.	Pretend you are preparing to write a report on where paper comes from. Create a graphic organizer that could help you keep track of the information you find in your research.	Draw a picture of a simple shape such as a star or heart. Cover your shape with tracing paper. Use dots along the outline of your shape to create an alphabet dot-to-dot puzzle in the order of *a* to *z.*	Imagine the perfect dinner and dessert. Write words to describe the foods you would eat. Write the descriptions on a paper plate.

Rain on the green grass,
And rain on the tree,
Rain on the housetop,
But not on me.

Draw a picture of what the child might be holding.

Match the letters.

A	c
C	b
E	e
B	a
D	d

Color the nouns.

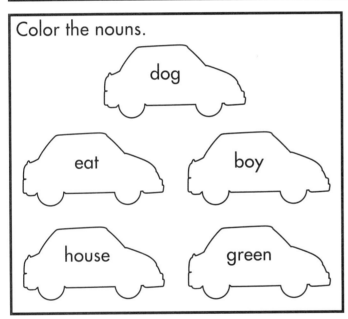

dog
eat
boy
house
green

Help put the doll in the toy box. Draw a line through the pictures whose names begin with **c**, as in cap.

Circle the number of syllables in each word.

cub	1	2	3
dog	1	2	3
tip	1	2	3

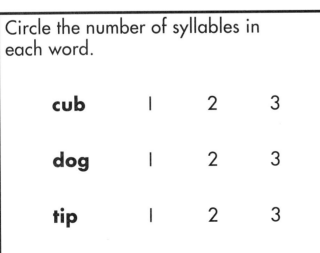

Color the word that names the picture.

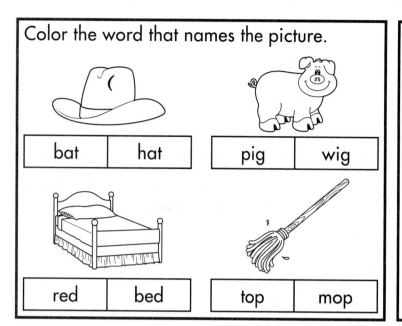

bat	hat

pig	wig

red	bed

top	mop

She _____ on the bed.

jumps

jumping

jump

Say. Connect. Write.

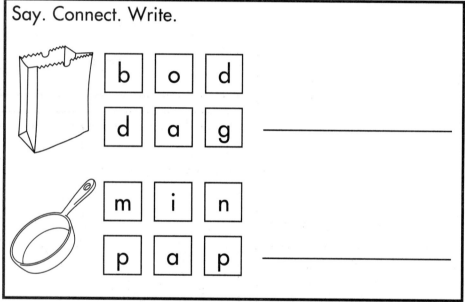

b	o	d

d	a	g

_____

m	i	n

p	a	p

_____

Trace.

Aa

Write.

Write an answer to the question in a complete sentence. Underline the capital letters in your sentence. Circle the ending punctuation.

What is your name?

_____

_____

Rewrite the sentence correctly.

mrs. brown is my teacher

_____

Sort the words.

blue   **one**   **red**

six   **three**   **white**

Colors	Numbers

Say the name of the picture. Choose the correct spelling.

○ **cub**

○ **cup**

○ **cap**

Write the letters to spell the word **any**.

an___   a___y

___ny

Use the word in a sentence.

_____

_____

Find the singular and plural forms of each word. Color them the same color.

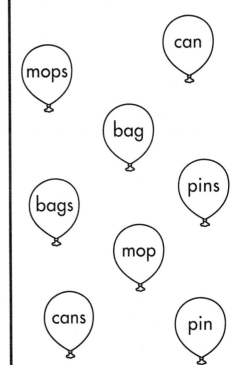

Use the words to write a sentence.

hen	the	sat

_____

Find and circle the words. There are two of each one.

came   **saw**   **with**

c   a   m   e   i   z   v   c
s   w   h   s   r   d   o   a
b   i   l   a   s   a   w   m
k   t   u   w   f   e   j   e
x   h   f   e   w   i   t   h

pot

lip

dog

Change the word by writing a different beginning letter on each line.

hat

_____at

_____at

_____at

The girl sees a dog. It is black. It has big ears. The dog jumps up and down. The girl and the dog play.

What color is the dog? _____

What do the girl and the dog do?

_____

_____

Draw a line to match each picture to the correct category.

swims   **flies**

Say the name of each picture. Write the letters of each word in the boxes.

Unscramble each **short a** word. Write the correct spelling.

mpa   _____

bca   _____

ath   _____

Use the text to complete the diagram.

A car has many parts. The part you see is the body. The body sits on the frame. The frame is held by the 4 wheels.

Draw lines to divide each word into syllables.

s t a r f i s h

p o p c o r n

b a c k p a c k

Use the letters to make words. Try to make one word with all of the letters.

a	i
n	r

_____   _____

_____   _____

The baby _____ in the

car seat.

sit

sits

sitting

Draw a line through the words in the **-ap** family.

cap	bag	rat
man	tap	sad
sat	can	map

Trace.

Bb - - - - - - -

Write.

- - - - - - - - -

- - - - - - - - -

- - - - - - - - -

Complete the graphic organizer.

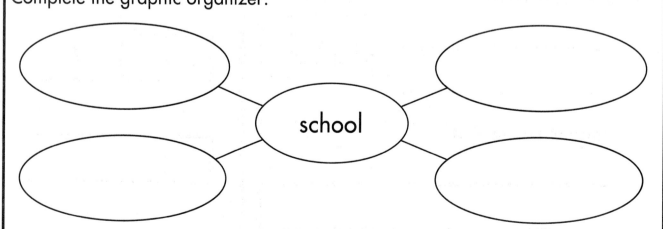

school

Say the name of each picture. Color the pictures that have the same vowel sound.

 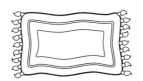

Connect the letters in ABC order. Start at the star.

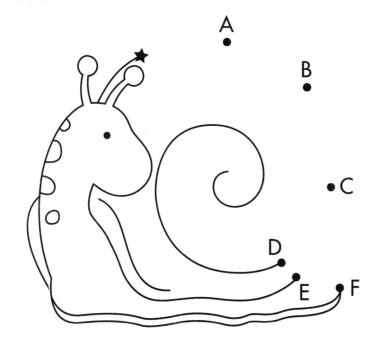

A

B

•C

D

E   •F

Draw an **X** through the word that does not belong.

two   **six**

ant   **ten**

A farm has a barn. A barn is red. Cows live in barns.

The author told me that

_____

_____.

The picture shows me that

_____

_____.

Write each sight word in the correct word shape.

came   **saw**   **with**

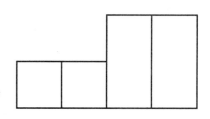

Use adjectives to expand the sentence.

I have a cap.

_____

_____

Write the word one letter at a time.

drum

_____

_____ _____

_____ _____ _____

_____ _____ _____ _____

hen

mug

pig

Trace the words using four colors.

of of

of of

of of

of of

Write a sentence that ends with a period. Use the word **on** in the sentence.

_____

_____

_____

_____

Star light, star bright,
First star I see tonight,
I wish I may, I wish I might,
Have the wish I wish tonight.

What is the child wishing on?

_____

_____

_____

Match the letters.

F   f

I   h

G   i

J   g

H   j

Color the nouns.

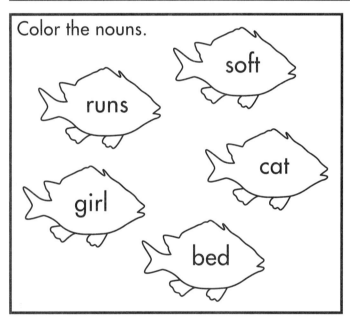

soft

runs

cat

girl

bed

Circle the number of syllables in each word.

cow   1   2

dress   1   2

pool   1   2

Say the name of each picture. Color the boxes that have words with **long a** sounds.

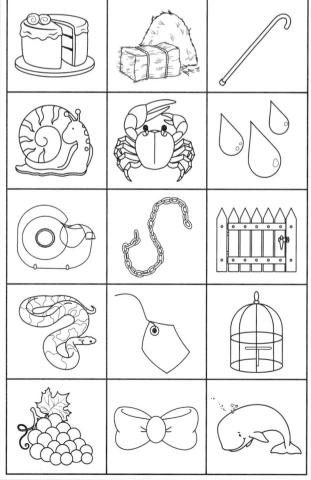

Color the word that names the picture.

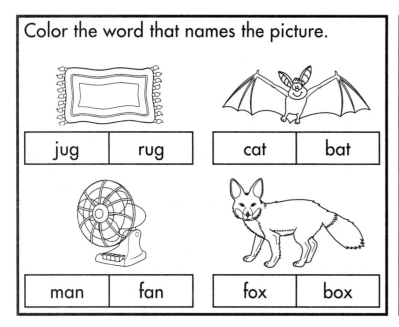

jug	rug

cat	bat

man	fan

fox	box

My dog _____ at cars.

bark

barking

barks

Say. Connect. Write.

c	u	t

d	a	l

_____

m	o	n

f	a	p

_____

Trace.

Cc

Write.

Write an answer to the question in a complete sentence. Underline the capital letter in your sentence. Circle the ending punctuation.

What is your favorite time of day? Why?

_____

_____

Rewrite the sentence correctly.

wild pandas are found only in china

_____

_____

Sort the words.

black   **four**   **nine**

orange   **two**   **yellow**

Colors	Numbers

Write the letters to spell the word **old**.

o_____d   ol_____

_____ld

Use the word in a sentence.

_____

_____

Say the name of the picture. Choose the correct spelling.

○ **bad**

○ **bed**

○ **bet**

Find the singular and plural forms of each word. Color them the same color.

cup

cat

log

cups

pens

cats

logs

pen

Use the words to write a sentence.

ran	dog	the

_____

Find and circle the words. There are two of each one.

have   **new**   **want**

c   n   f   r   h   a   v   e
w   e   h   h   r   f   h   j
a   w   l   a   v   n   e   w
n   r   u   v   w   a   n   t
t   g   p   e   r   l   z   c

hat

egg

bag

Change the word by writing a different beginning letter on each line.

dig

_____ig

_____ig

_____ig

My bike is blue. My bike has a bell. I ring the bell. I like to ride my bike at the park. I go fast.

What color is the bike? _____

Where does the child ride his or her bike?

_____

_____

Name _____

Draw a line to match each picture to the correct category.

red   **green**

Say the name of each picture. Write the letters of each word in the boxes.

Unscramble each **short e** word. Write the correct spelling.

neh   _____

nte   _____

edb   _____

Draw lines to divide each word into syllables.

a n t h i l l

b a s e b a l l

b a t h t u b

Ethan's Chores

Day 1   make bed

Day 2   mop

Day 3   walk dog

Day 4   set table

Day 5   mop

What chore does Ethan do on Day 1?

_____

On what days does Ethan mop?

_____

_____

Name _____

Use the letters to make words. Try to make one word with all of the letters.

a	e
m	n

_____ _____

_____ _____

The pigs _____ in mud.

rolling

rolls

roll

Draw a line through the words in the **-am** family.

sad	mat	jam
wax	tag	ham
word	pad	yam

Trace.

Dd _ _ _ _

Write.

_ _ _ _ _ _ _

_____

_ _ _ _ _ _ _

_____

Complete the graphic organizer.

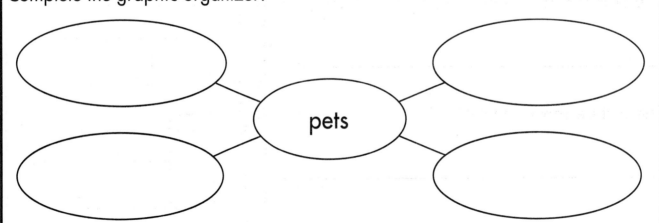

pets

Say the name of each picture. Color the pictures that have the same vowel sound.

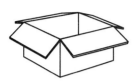   

Connect the letters in ABC order. Start at the star.

G ★

H •   • L

I •   J •   K •

Draw an **X** through the word that does not belong.

red   **bat**

green   **blue**

Many fish live in the sea. Some fish are big. Some fish are small.

The author told me that

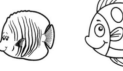

_____.

The picture shows me that

_____.

Write each sight word in the correct word shape.

have   **new**   **want**

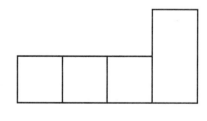

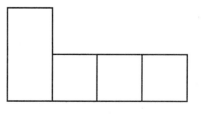

Use adjectives to expand the sentence.

My cat likes food.

_____

_____

Write the word one letter at a time.

frog

_____

_____ _____

_____ _____ _____

_____ _____ _____ _____

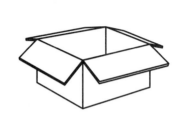

cup

pin

box

Trace the words using four colors.

had

had

had

had

Write a sentence that ends with a period. Use the word **up** in the sentence.

_____

_____

_____

_____

_____

Hickory, dickory, dock,
The mouse ran up the clock.
The clock struck one,
The mouse ran down,
Hickory, dickory, dock.

What made the mouse run down the clock?

_____

_____

_____

Match the letters.

M   k

O   o

L   n

K   l

N   m

Color the nouns.

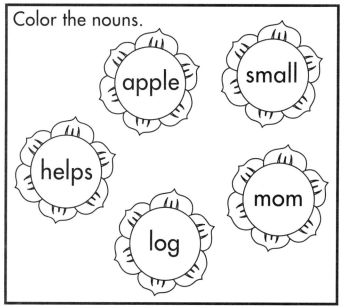

apple   small

helps

log   mom

Help the monkey find the bananas. Draw a line through the pictures whose names begin with **p**, as in pot.

Circle the number of syllables in each word.

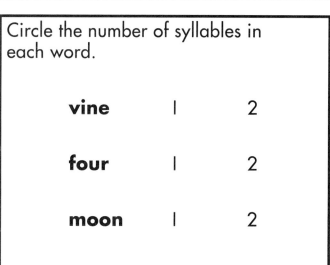

vine   1   2

four   1   2

moon   1   2

Color the word that names the picture.

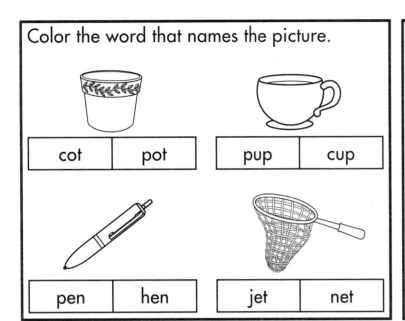

cot	pot

pup	cup

pen	hen

jet	net

Two friends _____ a game.

plays

playing

play

Say. Connect. Write.

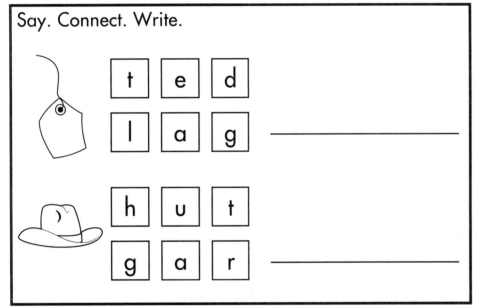

t	e	d

l	a	g	_____

h	u	t

g	a	r	_____

Trace.

E e

Write.

_____

- - - - - - - - - - - -

_____

- - - - - - - - - - - -

_____

Write an answer to the question in a complete sentence. Underline the capital letters in your sentence. Circle the ending punctuation.

Who are the people in your family?

_____

_____

Rewrite the sentence correctly.

i was born on the fourth of april

_____

Sort the words.

brown   **five**   **green**

one   **pink**   **two**

Colors	Numbers

Say the name of the picture. Choose the correct spelling.

○ **pin**

○ **pen**

○ **pig**

Write the letters to spell the word **ask**.

as____   a____k

____sk

Use the word in a sentence.

_____

_____

Find the singular and plural forms of each word. Color them the same color.

 bed
 net
 ant
 dogs
 nets
 dog
 beds
 ants

Use the words to write a sentence.

Tom	ball	plays

_____

Find and circle the words. There are two of each one.

of   **had**   **her**

c	h	e	r	h	o	b	p
s	i	h	h	r	f	h	j
o	f	l	a	v	s	a	a
k	r	u	d	w	m	d	f
f	g	h	e	r	l	z	c

dog

cat

bird

Change the word by writing a different beginning letter on each line.

dad

_____ad

_____ad

_____ad

   A cat is by the window. First, it sits and sits. It likes the sunny spot. Then, it naps and naps. The cat is happy.

How does the cat feel?

happy   **sad**   **mad**

What does the cat do at the end of the story?

sit   **nap**   **eat**

Name _____ **Week 6, Day 1**

Draw a line to match each picture to the correct category.

kitchen   **bathroom**

Say the name of each picture. Write the letters of each word in the boxes.

Unscramble each **short i** word. Write the correct spelling.

gwi _____

nip _____

idp _____

Use the text to complete the diagram.

This is a map of a room. The bed is near the door. The toy box is next to the chair. The rug is in the middle.

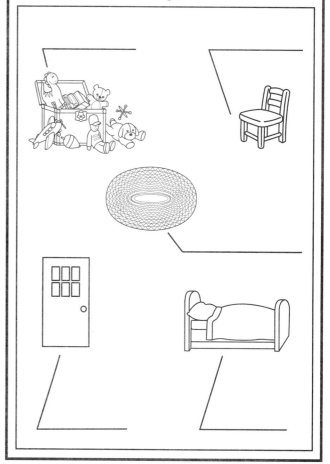

Draw lines to divide each word into syllables.

b o x c a r

f i s h b o w l

p o l i c e

© Carson-Dellosa • CD-104875

37

Use the letters to make words. Try to make one word with all of the letters.

n	o
s	w

_____ _____

_____ _____

The plant _____ to be

4 feet tall.

growing

grow

will grow

Circle the words in the **-ab** family.

bat	tag	dad
tab	cab	jab
ram	fan	cat

Trace.

F f _ _ _ _ _ _

Write.

_ _ _ _ _ _ _

_ _ _ _ _ _ _

Complete the graphic organizer.

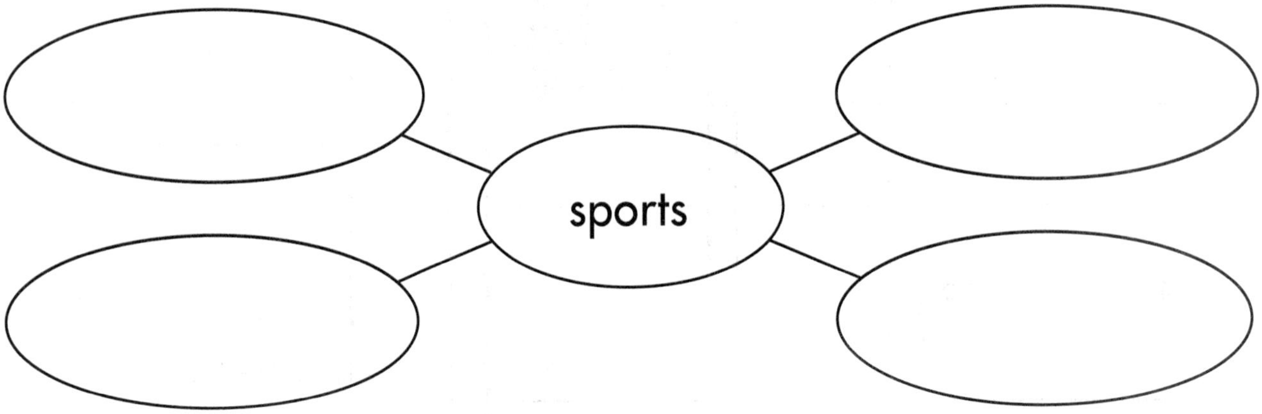

sports

Say the name of each picture. Color the pictures that have the same vowel sound.

Connect the letters in ABC order. Start at the star.

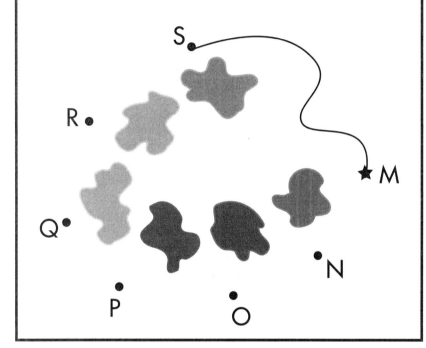

Draw an **X** through the word that does not belong.

hen   **five**

cow   **goat**

Write each sight word in the correct word shape.

of   **had**   **her**

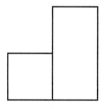

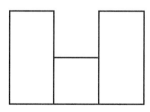

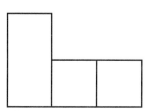

Animals live in many different places. Some animals live in trees. Some animals live in water. Some animals live underground.

The author told me that

_____

_____.

The picture shows me that

_____

_____.

Use adjectives to expand the sentence.

Jill has a bike.

_____

_____

Write the word one letter at a time.

doll

_____

_____   _____

_____   _____   _____

_____   _____   _____   _____

cap

fan

bag

Trace the words using four colors.

her

her

her

her

Write a sentence that ends with a period. Use the word **to** in the sentence.

_____

_____

_____

_____

_____

Baa, baa, black sheep, have you any wool?
Yes, sir, yes, sir, three bags full.
One for my master, one for my dame,
And one for the little boy who lives down
   the lane.

Who will get a bag of wool from the sheep?

_____

_____

_____

Match the letters.

P	q
S	t
T	r
Q	p
R	s

Color the nouns.

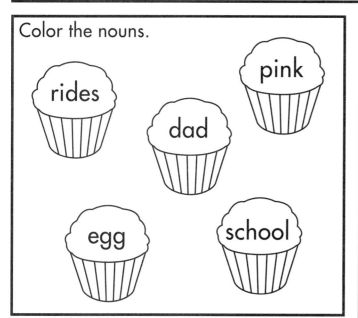

Circle the number of syllables in
each word.

handbag	1	2
flag	1	2
sandbox	1	2

Say the name of each picture. Color
the boxes that have words with
long e sounds.

Color the word that names the picture.

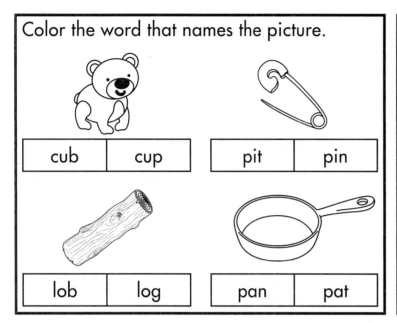

cub	cup

pit	pin

lob	log

pan	pat

The frogs _____ on

the log.

hops

hop

hopping

Say. Connect. Write.

b	e	p
k	i	d

_____

m	e	n
h	i	p

_____

Trace.

Gg

Write.

Write an answer to the question in a complete sentence. Underline the capital letter in your sentence. Circle the ending punctuation.

What is your favorite thing to wear? Why?

_____

_____

Rewrite the sentence correctly.

the ocean is home to fish turtles and whales _____

_____

Sort the words.

tree   **rug**   **fork**

ant   **cloud**   **bed**

Inside	Outside

Write the letters to spell the word **take**.

t___ke   tak___

ta___e   ___ake

Use the word in a sentence.

_____

_____

Say the name of the picture. Choose the correct spelling.

○ **pop**

○ **pit**

○ **pot**

Find the singular and plural forms of each word. Color them the same color.

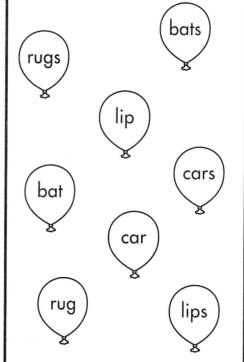

Use the words to write a sentence.

is	the	here	sled

_____

Find and circle the words. There are two of each one.

his　　**some**　　**as**

a	t	h	y	h	i	s	p
s	r	i	l	r	a	n	s
b	k	s	d	a	s	d	o
s	o	m	e	w	m	w	m
x	g	f	t	b	l	z	e

tent

ring

frog

Change the word by writing a different beginning letter on each line.

call

_____all

_____all

_____all

　　I see a bug. It is green and black. The bug goes up the tree. The bug is on a leaf. The bug eats the leaf. The bug goes down the tree. I see the bug on me!

What does the bug eat?

the tree　　　**me**　　　**the leaf**

Draw a picture of the bug.

44

Draw a picture for each word.

new	**old**

Say the name of each picture. Write the letters of each word in the boxes.

Unscramble each **short o** word. Write the correct spelling.

gof   _____

opt   _____

hto   _____

Draw lines to divide each word into syllables.

p i g p e n

s e a s h o r e

p a n c a k e

Use the chart to answer the questions.

Train A 8:00   New City

Train B 9:00   North Town

Train C 10:00   West Way

Train D 11:00   New City

Which trains go to New City?

_____

_____

Where might you find this chart?

_____

_____

Use the letters to make words. Try to make one word with all of the letters.

a	b	e	l	t

_____   _____

_____   _____

_____   _____

The boys _____ muffins

for the bake sale.

making

makes

make

Circle the words in the **-ed** family.

bed	net	leg
red	gem	ten
fed	pen	jet

Trace.

Write.

Complete the graphic organizer.

the farm

Say the name of each picture. Color the pictures that have the same vowel sound.

Draw a page that might appear in a nonfiction book about animals.

Draw an **X** through the word that does not belong.

shoe   **sock**

cup   **hat**

Write each sight word in the correct word shape.

as   **his**   **some**

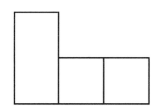

Frogs live in ponds. They lay eggs in the water. The eggs hatch. Baby frogs look like fish.

The author told me that

_____

_____.

The picture shows me that

_____.

Use adjectives to expand the sentence.

He ate an apple.

_____

_____

Write the word one letter at a time.

door

_____

_____ _____

_____ _____ _____

_____ _____ _____ _____

cow

tape

fork

Trace the words using four colors.

then

then

then

then

Write a sentence that ends with a period. Use the word **by** in the sentence.

_____

_____

_____

_____

There was an old woman
Who lived in a shoe.
She had so many children
She didn't know what to do;
She gave them some broth
Without any bread;
She kissed them all soundly
And put them to bed.

Do you think that a shoe makes a good home?

Explain. _____

_____

Match the letters.

V	X
U	U
X	V
Z	Y
W	W
Y	z

Color the nouns.

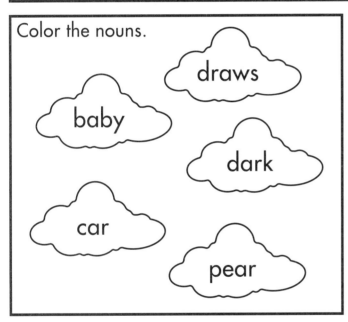

draws
baby
dark
car
pear

Help the bears find their home. Draw a line through the pictures whose names begin with **l**, as in lamp.

Circle the number of syllables in each word.

stamp	1	2
shoelace	1	2
zipper	1	2

Color the word that names the picture.

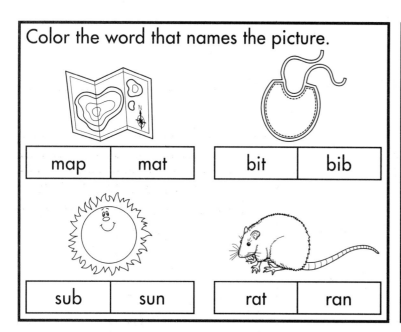

map	mat

bit	bib

sub	sun

rat	ran

Helen _____ fast on ice.

skates

skating

skate

Say. Connect. Write.

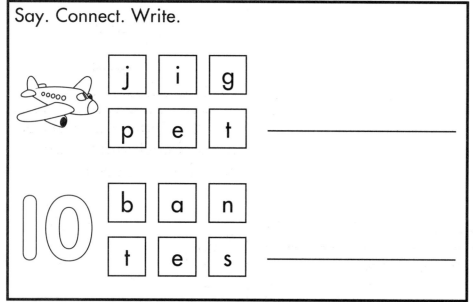

j	i	g

| p | e | t | _____
|---|---|---|

b	a	n
t	e	s	_____

Trace.

Ii

Write.

Write an answer to the question in a complete sentence. Underline the capital letter in your sentence. Circle the ending punctuation.

What do you do to make a sad friend feel better?

_____

_____

Rewrite the sentence correctly.

jane rides around the park but jed runs around the park _____

_____

Sort the words.

boy   **pin**   **mom**

book   **hat**   **baby**

Objects	People

Say the name of the picture. Choose the correct spelling.

○ **hug**

○ **mug**

○ **mud**

Write the letters to spell the word **then**.

t_____en   the_____

_____hen   th_____n

Use the word in a sentence.

_____

_____

Find the singular and plural forms of each word. Color them the same color.

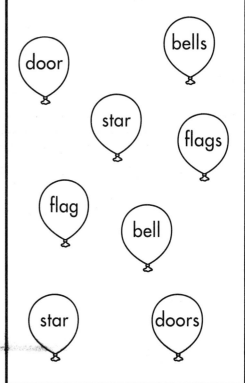

Use the words to write a sentence.

ate	the	I	apple

_____

Find and circle the words. There are two of each one.

could   him   then

c	t	h	e	n	u	b	p
o	i	h	s	r	h	i	m
u	k	i	c	o	u	l	d
l	r	m	t	w	m	w	f
d	g	f	e	t	h	e	n

comb

plate

bike

Change the word by writing a different vowel on each line.

pan

p_____n

p_____n

p_____n

It is a hot, sunny day. The pool looks so cool. The kids jump in and swim. Water splashes out. The kids swim under the water. They get out to rest.

What is the weather like?

cool   hot   rainy

What do the kids do in the pool?

swim   rest   look

Draw a picture for each word.

neat	**messy**

Say the name of each picture. Write the letters of each word in the boxes.

Unscramble each **short u** word. Write the correct spelling.

sbu _____

tuc _____

umg _____

What do you like to eat? Maybe you like sweet foods. Cake is sweet. Maybe you like salty foods. Chips are salty. The areas of your tongue sense different tastes.

Color the areas of the tongue.

red = sweet
orange = salty
yellow = sour
blue = bitter

Draw lines to divide each word into its syllables.

r a i n c o a t

s u i t c a s e

a i r p o r t

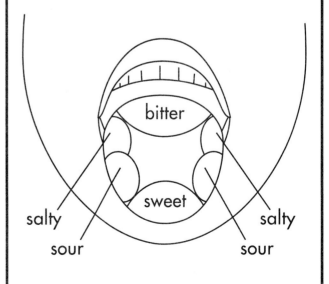

Use the letters to make words. Try to make one word with all of the letters.

a	e	r	t	w

_____   _____

_____   _____

_____   _____

They will _____ the mess

at the table.

cleaning

cleans

clean

Circle the words in the **-en** family.

red	wet	hen
hem	ten	set
pen	jet	led

Trace.

Jj

Write.

_____

_____

_____

_____

Complete the graphic organizer.

weather

Say the name of each picture. Color the pictures that have the same vowel sound.

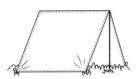   

Connect the letters in ABC order. Start at the star.

W
•

V •   • X

U •   • Y

T ★   • Z

Draw an **X** through the word that does not belong.

doll   **bee**

truck   **ball**

Write each sight word in the correct word shape.

could   him   then

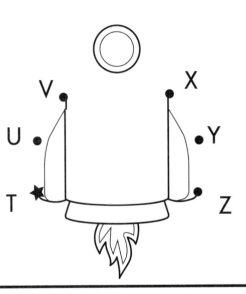

Oranges are fruit. There are many different kinds of oranges. They start out green. They turn orange when they are ripe.

The author told me that

_____

_____ .

The picture shows me that

_____ .

Use adjectives to expand the sentence.

They will watch a movie.

_____

_____

Write the word one letter at a time.

fire

_____

_____   _____

_____   _____   _____

_____   _____   _____   _____

muffin

house

sock

Trace the words using four colors.

were

were

were

were

Write a sentence that ends with a period. Use the word **off** in the sentence.

_____

_____

_____

_____

Draw a line to match each word to the correct category.

Goldilocks

house   **character**

Papa Bear   **setting**

woods

Write the words in ABC order.

food   _____

water   _____

space   _____

air   _____

needs   _____

Color the nouns.

park

teacher

hides

hot

sock

Say the name of each picture. Color the boxes that have words with **long i** sounds.

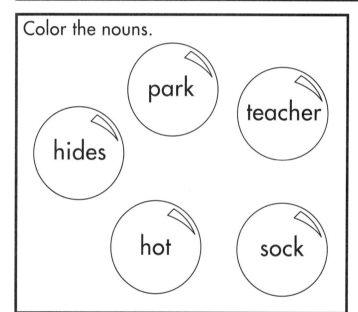

Circle the number of syllables in each word.

necklace   1   2

paint   1   2

hammer   1   2

Color the word that names the picture.

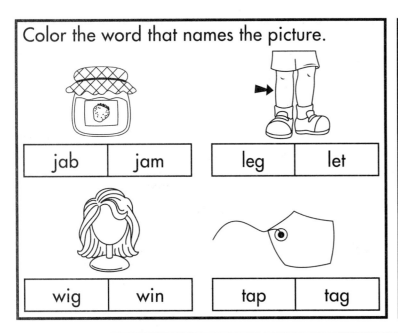

jab	jam

leg	let

wig	win

tap	tag

Sara _____ a picture of her cat.

paint

paints

painting

Say. Connect. Write.

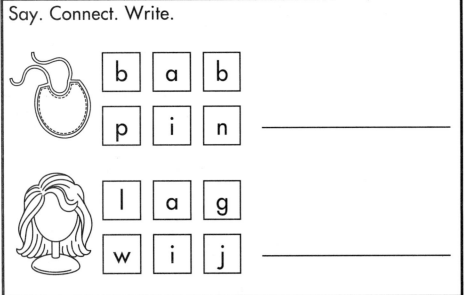

b	a	b
p	i	n

_____

l	a	g
w	i	j

_____

Trace.

Write.

Write an answer to the question in a complete sentence. Underline the capital letter in your sentence. Circle the ending punctuation.

What is your favorite thing to do at recess? Why?

_____

_____

Rewrite the sentence correctly.

yesterday was hot but today is hotter _____

_____

Sort the words.

park   **home**   **glue**

ring   **school**   **car**

Places	Objects

Write the letters to spell the word **over**.

ov___ r   ___ ver

o ___ er   ove ___

Use the word in a sentence.

_____

_____

Say the name of the picture. Choose the correct spelling.

○ **batt**

○ **bat**

○ **bate**

Find the singular and plural forms of each word. Color them the same color.

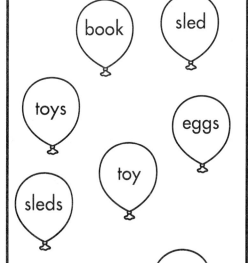

Use the words to write a sentence.

hat	that	big	is	a

_____

Find and circle the words. There are two of each one.

ask   **over**   **when**

c	w	h	e	n	u	b	a
a	o	j	o	v	e	r	s
s	v	l	d	c	s	d	k
k	e	u	t	w	h	e	n
x	r	f	e	b	l	z	c

Circle the word that is a proper noun.

girl

Katie

teacher

Change the word by writing a different vowel on each line.

born

b_____rn

b_____rn

After school, Matt goes home to feed his pet. Pat is Matt's pet fish. Pat swims fast when he sees Matt. Matt gives Pat fish food. Matt is happy to see Pat eat and swim.

Who is Pat?

a boy   **a girl**   **a fish**

What does Pat do when he sees Matt?

jumps   **swims**   **talks**

Draw a picture for each word.

wet | **dry**

Say the name of each picture. Write the letters of each word in the boxes.

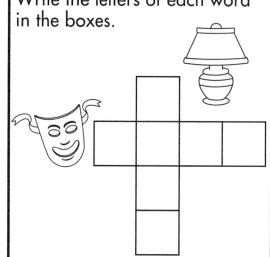

Unscramble each **long a** word. Write the correct spelling.

kace   _____

tega   _____

enac   _____

A-tisket a-tasket
A green and yellow basket
I wrote a letter to my love
And on the way I dropped it,
I dropped it,
I dropped it,
And on the way I dropped it.
A little boy he picked it up and put it
     in his pocket.

Draw a picture of the basket.

Draw lines to divide each word into syllables.

b u t t e r

s u m m e r

r a b b i t

Use the letters to make words. Try to make one word with all of the letters.

a	b	d	e	r

_____   _____

_____   _____

_____   _____

Mom _____ good

stories.

telling

tells

tell

Draw a line through the words in the **-ip** family.

wig	dip	bib
kit	lip	pig
lid	tip	him

Trace.

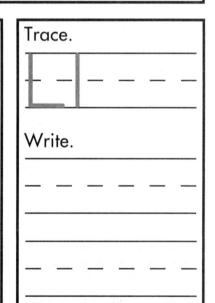

Write.

- - - - - - -

_____

- - - - - - -

_____

Draw the steps in the graphic organizer.

Washing Your Hands

☐ → ☐ → ☐ → ☐

Say the name of each picture. Color the pictures that have the same vowel sound.

Connect the letters in ABC order. Start at the star.

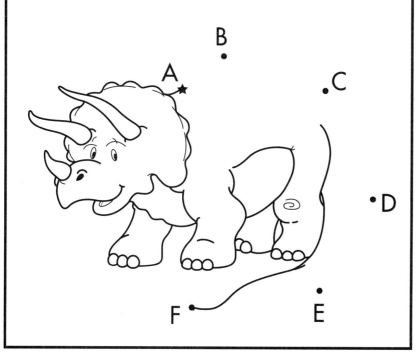

Draw an **X** through the word that does not belong.

car   truck

rug   bus

Ladybugs live in many places. They like forests. Ladybugs do not like the cold. They hide in warm places such as under rocks and logs.

The author told me that

_____

_____.

The picture shows me that

_____.

Write each sight word in the correct word shape.

ask   over   when

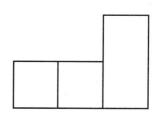

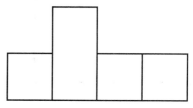

Use adjectives to expand the sentence.

It is raining.

_____

_____

Write the word one letter at a time.

time

_____

_____ _____

_____ _____ _____

_____ _____ _____ _____

Circle the word that is a proper noun.

brother

car

Sam

Trace the words using four colors.

ask

ask

ask

ask

Write a sentence that ends with a period. Use the word **with** in the sentence.

_____

_____

_____

_____

_____

Draw a line to match each word to the correct category.

Gingerbread Boy

town

river

fox

character

setting

Write the words in ABC order.

root _____

plant _____

stem _____

leaf _____

flower _____

Color the adjectives.

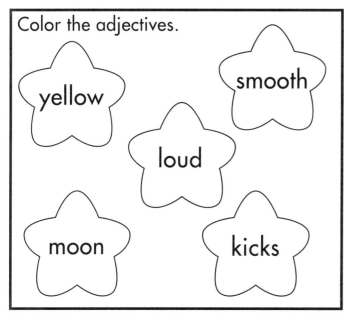

yellow

smooth

loud

moon

kicks

Twinkle, twinkle, little star,
How I wonder what you are!
Up above the world so high,
Like a diamond in the sky.

Why is the star compared to a diamond?

_____

_____

_____

_____

_____

_____

Circle the number of syllables in each word.

thumb   1   2

donkey   1   2

notebook   1   2

Color the word that names the picture.

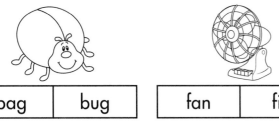

bag	bug

fan	fin

lap	lip

pan	pin

They _____ three parks.

visit

visits

visiting

Say. Connect. Write.

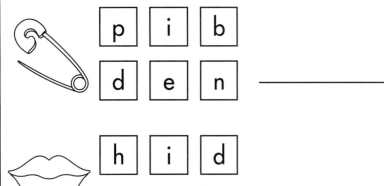

p	i	b
d	e	n

_____

h	i	d
l	a	p

_____

Trace.

Mm

Write.

_____

_____

_____

Write an answer to the question in a complete sentence. Underline the capital letter in your sentence. Circle the ending punctuation.

Do you like to do work in a noisy room or a quiet room? Why?

_____

_____

Rewrite the sentence correctly.

what is brown and sticky _____

_____

A stick!

Sort the words.

cake   **jump**   **run**

nail   **talk**   **spider**

Nouns	Verbs

Say the name of the picture. Choose the correct spelling.

○ **cake**

○ **cak**

○ **kake**

Find the singular and plural forms of each word. Color them the same color.

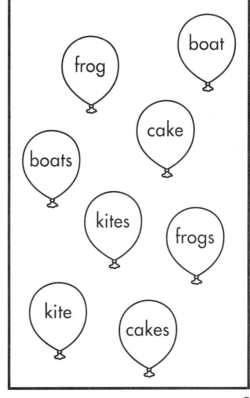

Write the letters to spell the word **from**.

f ___ om   ___ rom

fro ___   fr ___ m

Use the word in a sentence.

_____

_____

Use the words to write a sentence.

car	the	we	see

_____

Find and circle the words. There are two of each one.

an   them   were

c   t   y   j   h   u   a   w
s   h   w   e   r   e   k   e
b   e   l   d   v   s   d   r
a   m   u   t   h   e   m   e
n   g   a   n   b   l   z   c

Circle the word that is a proper noun.

store

Mr. Lee

game

Change the word by writing a different vowel on each line.

bill

b_____ll

b_____ll

b_____ll

Ann has a book. Her grandma reads with her. They read the book on the couch. Ann can read some words. Her grandma helps her read new words. After they read, Ann picks another book.

Where do Ann and her grandma read?

table   chair   couch

Who helps Ann read a book?

dad   grandma   sister

Name _____ Week 14, Day 1

Draw a picture for each word.

fast | **slow**

Say the name of each picture. Write the letters of each word in the boxes.

Unscramble each **long i** word. Write the correct spelling.

iveh _____

tkie _____

ebki _____

Use the text to complete the diagram.

Insects have many parts. Their bodies have three sections: the abdomen, thorax, and head. They have six legs. Some insects have wings.

Draw lines to divide each word into syllables.

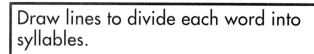

y e l l o w

w a l l e t

z i p p e r

© Carson-Dellosa • CD-104875

Name ______________________________ **Week 14, Day 2**

Use the letters to make words. Try to make one word with all of the letters.

e	h	o	r	s

______________ ______________

______________ ______________

______________ ______________

Ms. May ____________ my cat last week.

watch

watched

will watch

Circle the words in the **-in** family.

big	kid	fit
rib	hit	bid
pin	fin	win

Trace.

Nn

Write.

Draw the steps in the graphic organizer.

Brushing Your Teeth

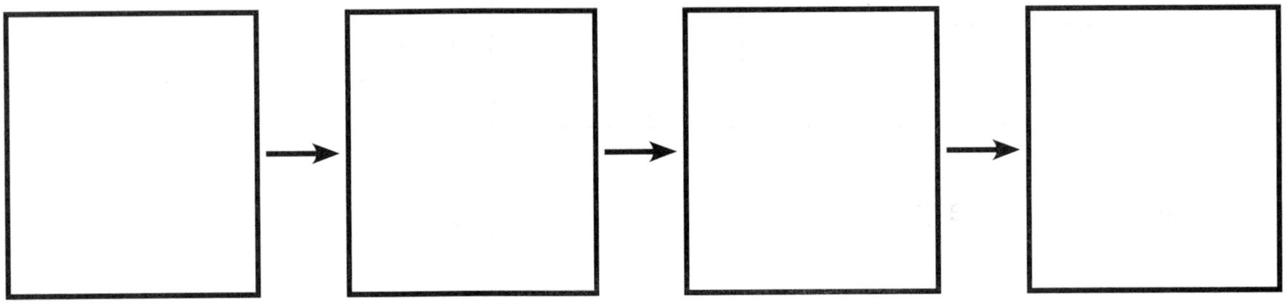

Say the name of each picture. Color the pictures that have the same vowel sound.

Connect the letters in ABC order. Start at the star.

J

I   K

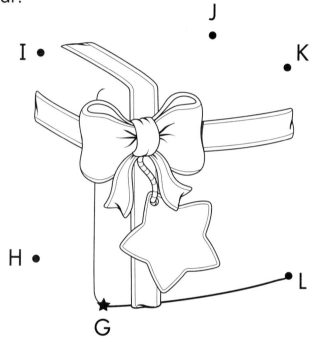

H   L

★
G

Draw an **X** through the word that does not belong.

pencil   owl

book   glue

Write each sight word in the correct word shape.

an   them   were

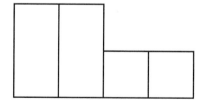

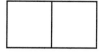

Sharks live in oceans. Sharks swim with their mouths open. This may look scary, but they are just breathing.

The author told me that

_____

_____.

The picture shows me that

_____.

Use adjectives to expand the sentence.

Charlie set the table.

_____

_____

Write the word one letter at a time.

bear

_____

_____ _____

_____ _____ _____

_____ _____ _____ _____

Circle the word that is a proper noun.

Dr. Gold

hat

pool

Trace the words using four colors.

over

over

over

over

Write a sentence that ends with a period. Use the word **from** in the sentence.

_____

_____

_____

_____

Draw a line to match each word to the correct category.

brick house

wolf   **character**

pig   **setting**

straw house

Write the words in ABC order.

lung   _____

frog   _____

egg   _____

hop   _____

gill   _____

Color the adjectives.

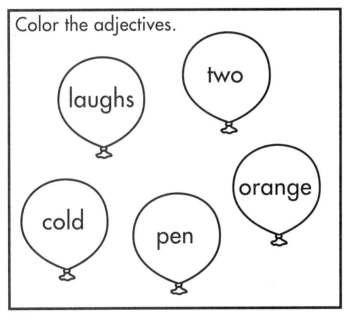

Circle the number of syllables in each word.

bookcase   1   2

grass   1   2

watch   1   2

Say the name of each picture. Color the boxes that have words with **long o** sounds.

Color the word that names the picture.

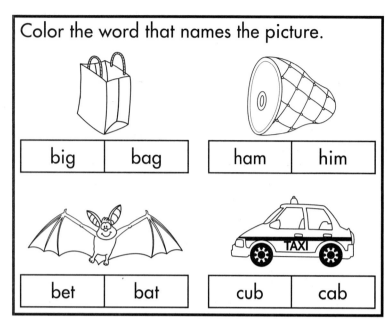

big	bag

ham	him

bet	bat

cub	cab

Dad _____ me two

books every night.

reads

reading

read

Say. Connect. Write.

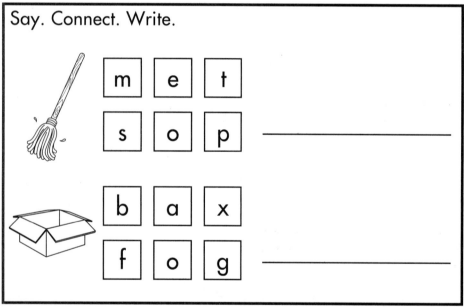

m	e	t

| s | o | p |
|---|---|---| _____

b	a	x

| f | o | g |
|---|---|---| _____

Trace.

Oo

Write.

Write an answer to the question in a complete sentence. Underline the capital letter in your sentence. Circle the ending punctuation.

What is your favorite toy? Why?

_____

_____

Rewrite the sentence correctly.

fish move their tails side to side _____

_____

Sort the words.

write   **ship**   **bread**

clean   **apple**   **throw**

Nouns	Verbs

Say the name of the picture.
Choose the correct spelling.

○ **bot**

○ **bote**

○ **boat**

Write the letters to spell the word **some**.

s____ me   ____ome

so____ e   som____

Use the word in a sentence.

_____

_____

Find the singular and plural
forms of each word. Color
them the same color.

 mules   drum

 mule   grill

 canes   cane

 drums   grills

Use the words to write a sentence.

| have | blue | i | a | cup |

_____

Find and circle the words. There are two of each one.

any   **how**   **just**

c t y o h u h p
a j u s t a o j
n k l a n y w u
y r u t w m q s
x h o w b l z t

Circle the word that is a proper noun.

baby

lion

Kelly

Change the word by writing a different vowel on each line.

male

m_____le

m_____le

m_____le

Scott plays on the playground. He gets on a swing. Scott swings up and down. Evan comes to see if Scott wants to play ball. Scott and his friend play ball. They pass the ball and throw it high. Scott has fun at the playground.

Who is Evan?

brother   **father**   **friend**

What is one thing that Scott does not do at the playground?

play ball   **draw**   **swing**

Draw a picture for each word.

short	**tall**

Say the name of each picture. Write the letters of each word in the boxes.

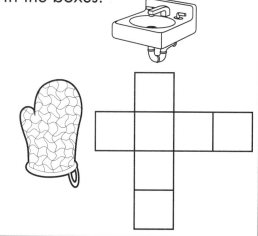

Unscramble each **long o** word. Write the correct spelling.

sheo   _____

ncoe   _____

epor   _____

I'm a little teapot, short and stout.
Here is my handle, here is my spout.
When I get all steamed up, hear me shout,
"Tip me over and pour me out!"

What is something the teapot does that people also do?

_____

_____

_____

_____

_____

Draw lines to divide each word into syllables.

r o b o t

t i g e r

p i l o t

Use the letters to make words. Try to make one word with all of the letters.

d	g	n	o	r	u

_____   _____

_____   _____

_____

He _____ across town to go to work.

driving

drive

drives

Circle the words in the **-ot** family.

hot	top	cob
mop	dot	box
job	bog	pot

Trace.

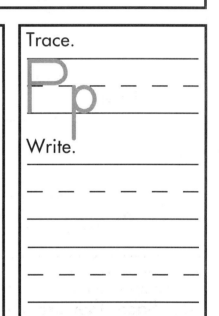

Write.

Draw the steps in the graphic organizer.

Building a Snowman

☐ → ☐ → ☐ → ☐

Say the name of each picture. Color the pictures that have the same vowel sound.

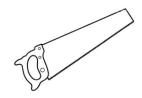 

Connect the letters in ABC order. Start at the star.

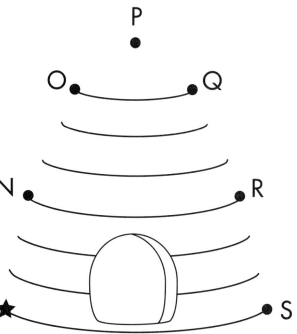

P

O   Q

N   R

M ★   S

Draw an **X** through the word that does not belong.

horse   **bed**

chair   **table**

Write each sight word in the correct word shape.

any   how   just

Bones are inside of your body. Bones give you shape. They are hard and strong. Bones keep your insides safe. Without bones, you would look like a floppy bag.

The author told me that

_____

_____ .

The picture shows me that

_____ .

Use adjectives to expand the sentence.

Mom lost her bag.

_____

_____

Write the word one letter at a time.

baby

_____

_____ _____

_____ _____ _____

_____ _____ _____ _____

Circle the word that is a proper noun.

Friday

week

month

Trace the words using four colors.

from

from

from

from

Write a sentence that ends with a period. Use the word **over** in the sentence.

_____

_____

_____

_____

Draw a line to match each word to the correct category.

giant

beanstalk   **character**

Jack   **setting**

castle

Write the words in ABC order.

ocean   _____

whale   _____

fish   _____

reef   _____

wave   _____

Color the adjectives.

truck

cries

bumpy

nine

quick

black

Circle the number of syllables in each word.

pepper   1   2

ring   1   2

flower   1   2

There was a little boy went into
    a barn
And lay down on some hay;
An owl came out and flew about,
And the little boy ran away.

What words tell you how the boy felt when he saw the owl?

_____

_____

_____

_____

Color the word that names the picture.

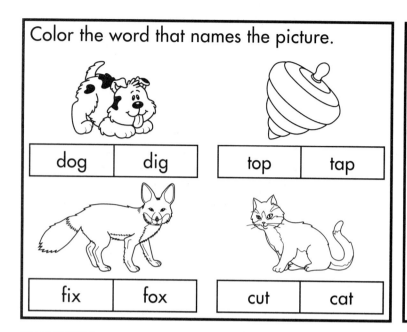

dog	dig

top	tap

fix	fox

cut	cat

The tigers _____ once a day.

eats

eating

eat

Say. Connect. Write.

d	o	g

l	a	p
_____

f	o	p

m	i	x
_____

Trace.

Write.

Write an answer to the question in a complete sentence. Underline the capital letter in your sentence. Circle the ending punctuation.

Would you like to fly like a bird or swim like a fish? Why?

_____

_____

Name _____

Rewrite the sentence correctly.

this cookie is for mommy but all of those with sprinkles are for me _____

_____

Sort the words.

she   **officer**   **you**

we   **grandma**   **boy**

Nouns	Pronouns

Say the name of the picture. Choose the correct spelling.

○ **tre**

○ **tree**

○ **trey**

Write the letters to spell the word **were**.

w____ re   ____ere

we____e   wer____

Use the word in a sentence.

_____

_____

Find the singular and plural forms of each word. Color them the same color.

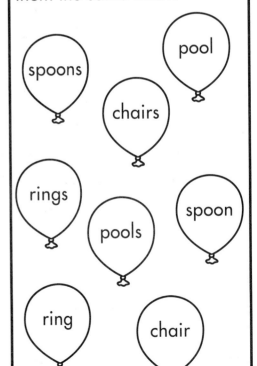

Name _____

Use the words to write a sentence.

| pizza | purple | two | monsters | ate |

_____

Find and circle the words. There are two of each one.

from   **know**   **put**

k   n   o   w   h   k   b   p
s   f   r   o   m   n   c   u
b   k   l   d   v   o   d   t
p   u   t   r   s   w   i   f
x   g   f   e   f   r   o   m

Circle the word that is a proper noun.

today

March

hour

Turn **bat** into **cup** by changing one letter at a time.

bat

_____at

ca_____

c_____p

I like the beach. The sand is soft and the water is cool. I splash and play all day. Then, Mom says, "It is time to go." I feel sad. I ask, "Can we come back tomorrow?"

How does the sand feel to the child?

_____

Why do you think that the child is sad when it is time to go?

_____

_____

Draw a picture for each word.

loose	**tight**

Say the name of each picture. Write the letters of each word in the boxes.

Unscramble each **long u** word. Write the correct spelling.

mleu _____

uecb _____

tuec _____

Draw lines to divide each word into syllables.

o p e n

s i l e n t

p a p e r

Many animals hibernate in the winter. Bears enter their dens in autumn and come out six to seven months later. Bats hibernate in caves. Frogs hibernate in mud at the bottoms of ponds. Groundhogs hibernate in burrows under the ground.

Draw a picture showing an animal hibernating. Write a caption for the picture.

Name ______________________________ Week 18, Day 2

Use the letters to make words. Try to make one word with all of the letters.

a	c	h	t	w

______________ ______________

______________ ______________

______________ ______________

The babies ____________ in the cribs.

napping

nap

naps

Circle the words in the **-ug** family.

nut	rub	cup
cub	hut	bud
rug	bug	mug

Trace.

Rr

Write.

Draw the steps in the graphic organizer.

Setting the Table

[ ] → [ ] → [ ] → [ ]

Say the name of each picture. Color the pictures that have the same vowel sound.

  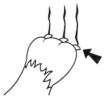 

Connect the letters in ABC order. Start at the star.

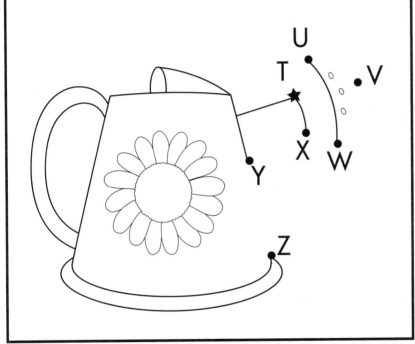

Draw an **X** through the word that does not belong.

square   **purple**

circle   **oval**

Write each sight word in the correct word shape.

from   **know**   **put**

Do you sneeze? Dust or germs can get in your nose. Your body makes you get rid of them. Your lung pushes air out and clears your nose.

The author told me that

_____

_____.

The picture shows me that

_____.

Use adjectives to expand the sentence.

Maddie has a game today.

_____

_____

Write the word one letter at a time.

back

_____

_____ _____

_____ _____ _____

_____ _____ _____ _____

Circle the word that is a proper noun.

town

home

New York City

Trace the words using four colors.

know

know

know

know

Write a sentence that ends with a period. Use the word **near** in the sentence.

_____

_____

_____

_____

Draw a line to match each word to the correct category.

dwarf

cottage   **character**

Snow White   **setting**

woods

Write the words in ABC order.

storm   _____

cloud   _____

rain   _____

snow   _____

wind   _____

Color the adjectives.

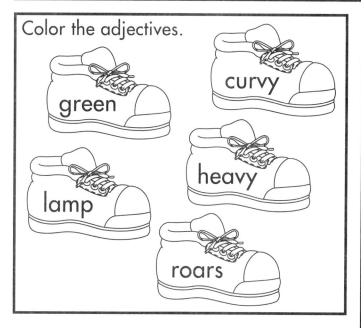

green

curvy

lamp

heavy

roars

Say the name of each picture. Color the boxes that have words with **long u** sounds.

Circle the number of syllables in each word.

teacher   1   2

chef   1   2

doctor   1   2

Color the word that names the picture.

slab	crab

train	stain

bread	tread

flag	drag

The girls _____ in the pool.

swims

swim

swimming

Say. Connect. Write.

b	u	p
g	o	s

_____

r	a	d
h	u	g

_____

Trace.

S s

Write.

Write an answer to the question in a complete sentence. Underline the capital letter in your sentence. Circle the ending punctuation.

Are you kind to others? Why?

_____

_____

Rewrite the sentence correctly.

the eiffel tower is in paris france _____

_____

Sort the words.

shoe   **soft**   **library**

peach   **quiet**   **purple**

Nouns	Adjectives

Write the letters to spell the word **give**.

_____ ive   g _____ve

giv _____   gi_____e

Use the word in a sentence.

_____

_____

Say the name of the picture. Choose the correct spelling.

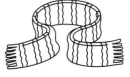

○ **skarf**

○ **skarff**

○ **scarf**

Find the singular and plural forms of each word. Color them the same color.

notes

cubes

hole

tree

note

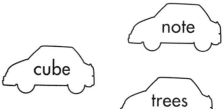

cube

trees

holes

Use the words to write a sentence.

| Ellie | today | went | school | to |

_____

Find and circle the words. There are two of each one.

every   **old**   **take**

c   t   y   j   e   u   b   p
o   l   d   s   v   a   o   t
b   t   a   k   e   s   l   a
k   r   u   t   r   m   d   k
e   v   e   r   y   l   c   e

Circle the word that is a proper noun.

Alaska

state

airplane

Turn **dog** into **hat** by changing one letter at a time.

dog

do_____

_____ot

h_____t

    Gina and her dad went to the store on Thursday. They put rice, beans, and milk in the cart. Her dad picked out a cookie for Gina. Gina picked out a bag of apples for Dad. They went to the front of the store to pay. Gina and her dad walked home to cook supper for their family.

Where did Gina and her dad go on Thursday?

_____

What did Gina and her dad buy at the store?

_____

_____

Draw a picture for each word.

quiet	**noisy**

Say the name of each picture. Write the letters of each word in the boxes.

Unscramble each **r-controlled vowel** word. Write the correct spelling.

bdir   _____

lirg   _____

irts   _____

Wee Willie Winkie
Runs through the town,
Upstairs and downstairs
In his nightgown,
Rapping at the window,
Crying through the lock,
"Are the children in their beds,
For now it's eight o'clock?"

What do you think Wee Willie Winkie should be doing? Why?

_____

_____

_____

_____

Draw lines to divide each word into syllables.

h a b i t

h u m a n

p r e t z e l

Use the letters to make words. Try to make one word with all of the letters.

a	e	l	p	p

_____   _____

_____   _____

_____   _____

The sun _____ through

the window.

shine

shines

shining

Circle the words that are nouns.

sad	run	hop
key	pencil	mug
cry	read	draw

Trace.

Write.

Draw the steps in the graphic organizer.

Planting a Seed

Say the name of each picture. Color the pictures that have the same vowel sound.

  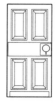 

Some plants catch insects and turn them into juice. The plants absorb the juice for food. A pitcher plant has leaves that look like a cup. The cup collects water. An insect crawls into the cup and drowns. Monkeys like to pick pitcher plants and drink the water inside.

Draw a line through the sentence in the text that does not help you know how some plants catch insects.

Draw an **X** through the word that does not belong.

apple   **bread**

fish   **bus**

Write each sight word in the correct word shape.

every   **old**   **take**

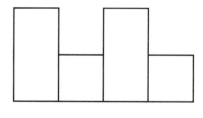

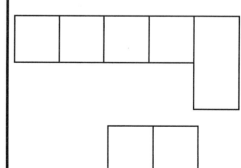

Bats are nocturnal animals. That means they sleep during the day and are awake at night. Bats sleep upside down.

The author told me that

_____

_____ .

The picture shows me that

_____ .

Rewrite the sentence to add more detail.

The mouse ate and went home.

_____

_____

Write the word one letter at a time.

house

____

____ ____

____ ____ ____

____ ____ ____ ____

____ ____ ____ ____ ____

Write a proper noun for the common noun.

store

_____

_____

Trace the words using four colors.

take

take

take

take

Write a sentence that ends with a question mark. Use the word **under** in the sentence.

_____

_____

_____

_____

Draw a line to match each word to the correct category.

Hansel

character

witch

setting

candy house

woods

Write the words in ABC order.

wheel   _____

axle   _____

pulley   _____

wedge   _____

lever   _____

Color the verbs.

swim

boat

run

yell

green

Match the word parts to complete the words.

rac   ter

des   coon

af   ert

Row, row, row your boat
Gently down the stream.
Merrily, merrily, merrily, merrily,
Life is but a dream.

How do you think the person in the boat feels? Why?

_____

_____

_____

_____

_____

Color the word that names the picture.

stop	drop

brick	trick

drip	slip

dress	press

I _____ my brother play

soccer later today.

watched

watch

will watch

Say. Connect. Write.

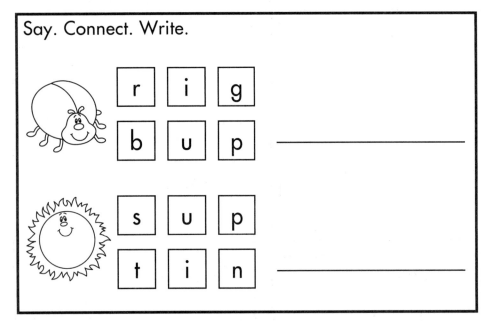

r	i	g
b	u	p

_____

s	u	p
t	i	n

_____

Trace.

U u

Write.

_ _ _ _ _ _ _

_____

_ _ _ _ _ _ _

_____

Write an answer to the question in a complete sentence. Underline the capital letter in your sentence. Circle the ending punctuation.

What would you do if one of your stuffed animals started talking to you?

_____

_____

Rewrite the sentence correctly.

what did one balloon say to another balloon at the party _____

_____

Watch out for the POPcorn!

Sort the words.

yellow   **spiky**   **leap**

lazy   **swim**   **cook**

Adjectives	Verbs

Write the letters to spell the word **just**.

____ust   ju____t

j____st   jus____

Use the word in a sentence.

_____

_____

Say the name of the picture. Choose the correct spelling.

◯ **gerl**

◯ **gurl**

◯ **girl**

Find the singular and plural forms of each word. Color them the same color.

 dresses
 bus

 dish
 brushes

 brush

 buses

dress

 dishes

Use the words to write a sentence.

| coat | is | that | my | yellow |

_____

Find and circle the words. There are two of each one.

after   **by**   **think**

t	a	c	a	h	u	b	y
h	f	p	f	r	a	o	l
i	t	d	t	h	i	n	k
n	e	s	e	c	m	b	f
k	r	o	r	h	x	y	g

Write a proper noun for the common noun.

day

_____

Turn **can** into **pet** by changing one letter at a time.

can

_____an

p_____n

pe_____

Lee and Sam are going hiking. The boys put on hats and boots. Lee brings a map, and Sam brings water. They hike a long way. Lee and Sam stop to rest. They hear twigs snap. All of a sudden, they see birds fly out of the trees. Lee and Sam decide to go back home.

What did the boys bring with them on their hike?

_____

What do you think makes the boys want to go back home?

_____

Draw a picture for each word.

open	**closed**

Say the name of each picture. Write the letters of each word in the boxes.

Unscramble each **r-controlled vowel** word. Write the correct spelling.

nfer _____

ursne _____

pseur _____

Draw lines to divide each word into syllables.

p a p e r

q u i c k l y

b a k e r

Sea otters have special parts that help them live in water. Their eyes and ears close under water. They have webbed feet to swim fast. Sea otters have thick fur. The fur traps air. It keeps them warm and dry.

Sea otters eat while floating on their backs. An otter places a rock on its chest. It smashes a shell against the rock. The shell cracks open and the otter eats the insides. Sea otters wash themselves after a meal. They need to keep their fur clean so that it stays waterproof.

What is the first paragraph about?

_____

What is the second paragraph about?

_____

Use the letters to make words. Try to make one word with all of the letters.

a	e	f	h	t	r

_____   _____

_____   _____

_____   _____

The artist _____ a

picture of our school tomorrow.

draws

draw

will draw

Circle the words that are verbs.

jelly	goat	hide
glad	talk	book
skip	pin	spoon

Trace.

V v

Write.

Write the beginning, middle, and end of a story.

Title: _____

_____

_____

_____

Beginning
↓
Middle
↓
End

Name _____ **Week 22, Day 3**

Say the name of each picture. Color the pictures that have the same vowel sound.

 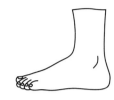  

Connect the letters in ABC order. Start at the star.

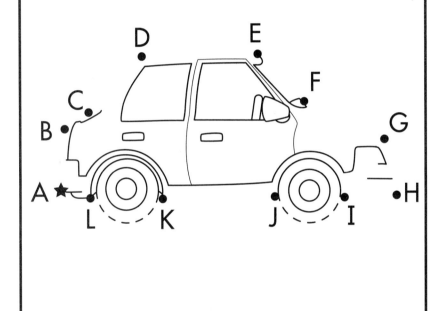

Draw an **X** through the word that does not belong.

goat   **horse**

shark   **goose**

Write each sight word in the correct word shape.

after   by   think

Animal ears are all different shapes. The shape is what helps the ear catch sounds from the air. The sounds go into your ear where a message is sent to your brain.

The author told me that

_____

_____.

The picture shows me that

_____.

© Carson-Dellosa • CD-104875

Rewrite the sentence to add more detail.

Gabby stepped into the water.

_____

_____

Write the word one letter at a time.

night

_____

_____ _____

_____ _____ _____

_____ _____ _____ _____

_____ _____ _____ _____ _____

Write a proper noun for the common noun.

movie

_____

_____

Trace the words using four colors.

walk

walk

walk

walk

Write a sentence that ends with an exclamation point. Use the word **above** in the sentence.

_____

_____

_____

_____

Draw lines to match the nouns and pronouns.

Henry   **it**

Mom and I   **he**

Mrs. Roberts   **she**

tree   **we**

Write the words in ABC order.

egg   _____

caterpillar _____

larva   _____

chrysalis   _____

butterfly   _____

Color the verbs.

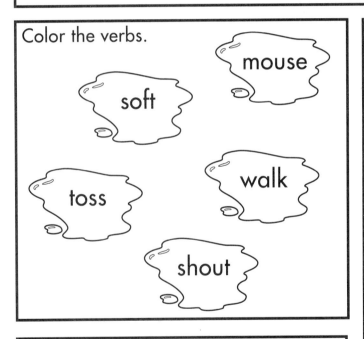

It's raining, it's pouring;
The old man is snoring.
Bumped his head
And he went to bed
And he couldn't get up in the
    morning.

Cross out the word from the poem that is not like the others. Explain how it is different.

snoring   **morning**

pouring   **raining**

_____

_____

_____

Match the word parts to complete the words.

gui   cher

sum   tar

tea   mer

Color the word that names the picture.

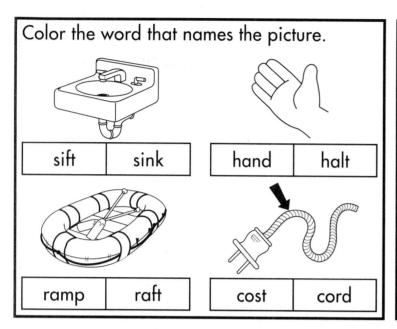

| sift | sink |
| hand | halt |

| ramp | raft |
| cost | cord |

She _____ the winning goal at last week's game.

kicked

kick

will kick

Say. Connect. Write.

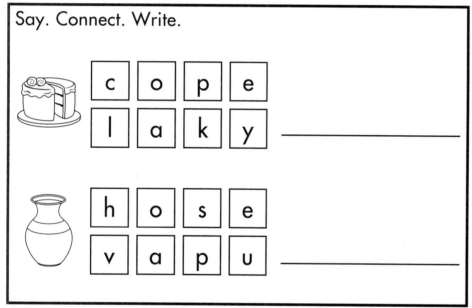

| c | o | p | e |
| l | a | k | y | _____

| h | o | s | e |
| v | a | p | u | _____

Trace.

W w

Write.

_____

_____

_____

_____

Write an answer to the question in a complete sentence. Underline the capital letter in your sentence. Circle the ending punctuation.

What is one thing you know about outer space?

_____

_____

Rewrite the sentence correctly.

you can here blood moving inside your head when you hold a shell to you're ear

_____

_____

Sort the words.

slowly   **silly**   **bright**

gently   **warm**   **quickly**

Adjectives	Adverbs

Write the letters to spell the word **open**.

ope____   op___n

____pen   o____en

Use the word in a sentence.

_____

_____

Say the name of the picture.
Choose the correct spelling.

◯ **leaf**

◯ **leef**

◯ **lefe**

Find the singular and plural
forms of each word. Color
them the same color.

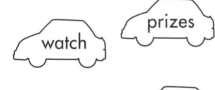
watch   prizes

prize   peaches

peach   watches

mile   miles

Use the words to write a sentence.

cannot	to	their	side	owls	side	eyes	move

_____

Find and circle the words. There are two of each one.

going   **let**   **walk**

c	g	y	w	w	a	l	k
s	o	h	a	s	l	e	t
b	i	l	l	d	g	d	a
k	n	u	k	t	l	e	t
x	g	o	i	n	g	z	c

Write a proper noun for the common noun.

town

_____

_____

Turn **leg** into **dot** by changing one letter at a time.

leg

l_____g

_____og

do_____

My baby brother always cries. He cries when he wakes up. He cries when he wants to eat. He cries when he wants to be held. I just want to play with him but he cries even more. One day, I will share my toys with him if he ever stops crying.

What is the problem?

_____

What would you tell the sister to do to stop her baby brother from crying?

_____

Draw a picture for each word.

shallow | **deep**

Say the name of each picture. Write the letters of each word in the boxes.

Unscramble each word. Write the correct spelling. Circle the digraph.

chlka _____

eyrrch _____

cchki _____

Write the prefix and base of each word.

review _____ _____

undo _____ _____

dislike _____ _____

Sloths are sluggish. Some sloths sleep up to 20 hours a day! They descend from the trees about once every week. Sloths move so slowly that even algae can grow on their fur. The algae growing on a sloth's fur helps it hide from predators. They blend in with green leaves.

What does **descend** mean?

_____

_____

Would a map of where sloths live be a good thing to include with this paragraph? Why or why not?

_____

_____

_____

Use the letters to make words. Try to make one word with all of the letters

a	d	e	g	n	r

_____   _____

_____   _____

_____   _____

The fox _____ the mouse and caught it.

chases

chased

will chase

Circle the words that are adjectives.

tape	cut	sharp
clap	bird	blue
bounce	lamp	angry

Trace.

X x ─ ─ ─ ─

Write.

─ ─ ─ ─ ─ ─

─ ─ ─ ─ ─ ─

─ ─ ─ ─ ─ ─

Write the beginning, middle, and end of a story.

Title: _____

_____

_____

_____

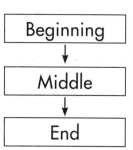

Say the name of each picture. Color the pictures that have the same vowel sound.

Rafflesia flowers grow in some rain forests. These flowers have no leaves or stems. Their five red petals can bloom as wide as a truck tire. Rafflesia flowers **attract** flies with the smell of rotting meat. The flies spread pollen to other rafflesia plants.

What could the author add to the text to help you say the name of the flower?

_____

Why is the word **attract** in bold?

_____

Draw an **X** through the word that does not belong.

ball   **bird**

bat   **mitt**

Write each sight word in the correct word shape.

going   **let**   **walk**

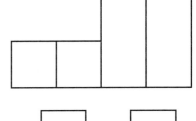

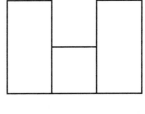

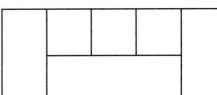

If a bone is broken, then you go see a doctor. If your car is broken, then you go see a mechanic. A mechanic helps fix cars and keep them running.

The author told me that

_____ .

The picture shows me that

_____ .

Rewrite the sentence to add more detail.

The ape swung on the tree.

_____

_____

Write the word one letter at a time.

thing

_____

_____ _____

_____ _____

_____ _____ _____

_____ _____ _____ _____

Write a proper noun for the common noun.

teacher

_____

_____

Trace the words using four colors.

stop

stop

stop

stop

Write a sentence that ends with a period. Use the word **inside** in the sentence.

_____

_____

_____

_____

_____

Name _____

Draw lines to match the nouns and pronouns.

house   it

Kayla and I   he

Mr. Lang   she

Lori   we

Write the words in ABC order.

subtract   _____

symbol   _____

equals   _____

number   _____

add   _____

Color the verbs.

Match the word parts to complete the words.

gar   tle

cir   den

lit   cle

Underline the past tense verbs in the poem.

There was a little turtle
Who lived in a box.
He swam in the puddles,
And he climbed on the rocks.

He snapped at the mosquito,
He snapped at the flea.
He snapped at the minnow,
And he snapped at me.

He caught the mosquito,
He caught the flea.
He caught the minnow,
But he didn't catch me!

Name _____

Color the word that names the picture.

chip	ship

whale	shale

thin	chin

thorn	shorn

She _____ a story about a pet cow.

write

wrote

writing

Say. Connect. Write.

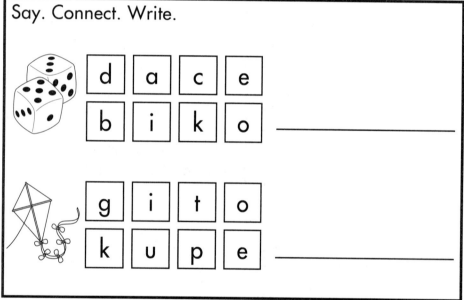

d	a	c	e

| b | i | k | o | _____
|---|---|---|---|

g	i	t	o

| k | u | p | e | _____
|---|---|---|---|

Trace.

Write.

Write an answer to each question in a complete sentence. Underline the capital letter in your sentence. Circle the ending punctuation.

What food do you wish tasted different? What would you like it to taste like? Why?

_____

_____

Rewrite the sentence correctly.

what has for wheels and flies _____

_____

A garbage truck!

Sort the words.

untie   **dislike**   **hopeful**

mistake   **careless**   **happier**

Words with Prefixes	Words with Suffixes

Say the name of the picture.
Choose the correct spelling.

○ **stule**

○ **stool**

○ **stoole**

Find the singular and plural forms of each word. Color them the same color.

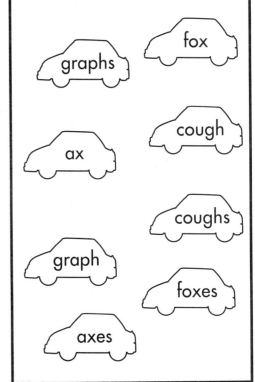

Write the letters to spell the word **know**.

kno____   kn____w

____now   k____ow

Use the word in a sentence.

_____

_____

Use the words to write a sentence.

| do | plants | how | food | make |

_____

Find and circle the words. There are two of each one.

again   **may**   **stop**

c	t	m	j	h	a	s	p
a	g	a	i	n	g	t	f
b	i	y	d	v	a	o	m
k	e	u	t	e	i	p	a
x	s	t	o	p	n	z	y

Write a proper noun for the common noun.

river

_____

_____

Turn **fan** into **cut** by changing one letter at a time.

fan

_____an

pa_____

_____at

c_____t

The library is Pam's favorite place to visit. She usually sits and reads two new books right when she walks in the door. Then, Pam goes to the computer and plays a game. Pam also enjoys checking out books to take home. She brings a bag to carry her library books. After reading, playing, and checking out new books, Pam is ready to go home.

What does Pam do as soon as she goes to the library?

_____

What does she do next?

_____

Draw a picture for each word.

careless	**careful**

Say the name of each picture. Write the letters of each word in the boxes.

Unscramble each word. Write the correct spelling. Circle the diagraph.

arksh _____

eflsh _____

shrti _____

How to Make a Fan

Materials:

• Sheet of paper

• Stapler

Directions:

1. Decorate both sides of a sheet of paper.

2. Start with one of the short edges. Fold the paper over and under in half-inch strips.

3. Hold one short end of the folded paper and staple it four times.

4. Spread the folds of the open end.

5. Hold the stapled end and move fan quickly to make "wind."

What could the author include to help the reader?

_____

_____

Draw lines to divide each word into syllables.

m i s s p e l l

r e p l a c e

u n k n o w n

Use the letters to make words. Try to make one word with all of the letters.

c	c	e	h	i	k	n

_____   _____

_____   _____

_____   _____

The bells _____ every hour.

ringing

rings

ring

Circle the words that should be capitalized.

tiger	day	couch
charlie	texas	july
girl	marker	stove

Trace.

Zz

Write.

_____
_ _ _ _ _ _ _
_____
_ _ _ _ _ _ _
_____

Write the beginning, middle, and end of a story.

Title: _____

_____

_____

_____

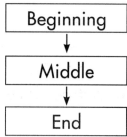

Beginning

↓

Middle

↓

End

Say the name of each picture. Color the pictures that have the same vowel sound.

Connect the letters in ABC order. Start at the star.

O P Q

R

S

T

W U

V

M N

Z X

Y

Draw an **X** through the word that does not belong.

scarf   gloves

towel   boots

Write each sight word in the correct word shape.

again   may   stop

What is a dream? A dream is a story that your brain creates. You may feel like you are really seeing and hearing things. Some dreams can be happy. Some dreams can be scary or sad. Dreams are only in your head.

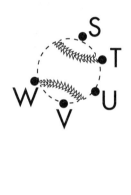

The author told me that

_____

_____.

The picture shows me that

_____.

Rewrite the sentence to add more detail.

Max was happy to read the book.

_____

_____

Write the word one letter at a time.

table

____

____ ____

____ ____ ____

____ ____ ____ ____

____ ____ ____ ____ ____

Write a proper noun for the common noun.

girl

_____

Trace the words using four colors.

give

give

give

give

Write a sentence that ends with a question mark. Use the word **beside** in the sentence.

_____

_____

_____

_____

_____

Draw lines to match the nouns and pronouns.

David's   her

Mom and Dad's   his

Lucy's   their

Draw a picture and write a caption for something that would appear in a nonfiction book about painting.

Color the verbs.

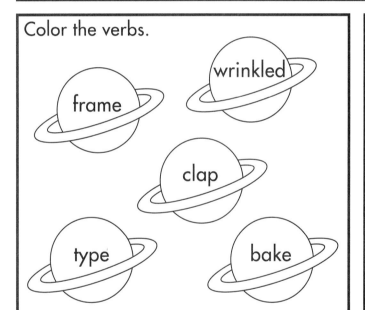

Little Boy Blue,
Come blow your horn,
The sheep's in the meadow,
The cow's in the corn;
Where is that boy
Who looks after the sheep?
Under the haystack,
Fast asleep.
Will you wake him?
Oh no, not I,
For if I do,
He will surely cry.

Write two words that describe Little Boy Blue.

_____

_____

Match the word parts to complete the words.

dis   heat

pre   lock

un   like

Color the word that names the picture.

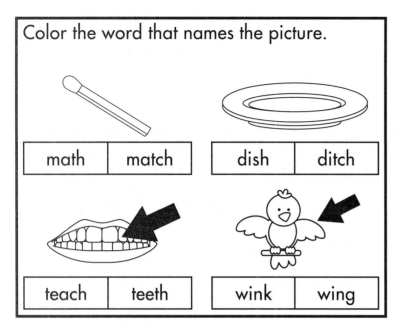

math	match

dish	ditch

teach	teeth

wink	wing

Mom and Dad _____

from home.

works

work

working

Say. Connect. Write.

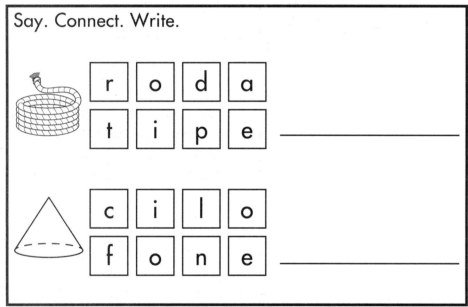

r	o	d	a
t	i	p	e	_____

c	i	l	o
f	o	n	e	_____

Say the name of the picture. Write the letters of the beginning sound.

_____

Write an answer to the question in a complete sentence. Underline the capital letter in your sentence. Circle the ending punctuation.

If you could switch places with a family member for one day, who would you switch places with? Why?

_____

_____

Rewrite the sentence correctly.

the first day of january is called new year's day _____

_____

Sort the words.

trying	**preview**	**useless**
kindness	**reread**	**unfair**

Words with Prefixes	Words with Suffixes

Say the name of the picture. Choose the correct spelling.

○ **fly**

○ **flie**

○ **fliy**

Find the singular and plural forms of each word. Color them the same color.

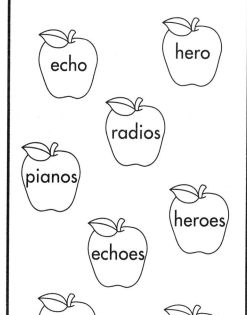

Write the letters to spell the word **when**.

whe_____   wh_____n

_____hen   w_____en

Use the word in a sentence.

_____

_____

Use the words to write a sentence.

| baby | cried | the | her | dropped | and | snack |

_____

_____

Find and circle the words. There are two of each one.

fly   **give**   **round**

c r o u n d b p
g i f s r f l y
i k l d v s w a
v r y r o u n d
e g i v e l z c

Write a proper noun for the common noun.

cereal

_____

_____

Turn **cup** into **hot** by changing one letter at a time.

cup

c_____p

ca_____

_____at

h_____t

"Something smells good," said Fran.

"I am making pizzas. Do you want to help?" asked Jake. Jake and Fran make three pizzas. Fran cuts up the toppings and Jake turns on the oven. They work together and put the toppings on the pizzas. Then, Jake puts them in the oven for ten minutes. Buzz! The timer is buzzing. The pizzas are ready!

Write a word that could replace **good** in the first sentence.

_____

How do you think Jake feels about Fran? How do you know?

_____

Draw a picture for each word.

narrow | **wide**

Say the name of each picture. Write the letters of each word in the boxes.

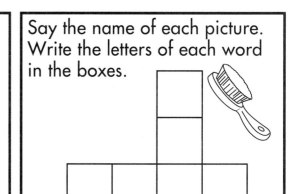

Unscramble each word. Write the correct spelling. Circle the digraph.

knath _____

rthee _____

umbth _____

Separate the suffix from the base word.

p a i n l e s s

d a r k n e s s

p e a c h e s

Giant squid have eyes the size of beach balls!

Owls spin their heads to see because they cannot move their eyes.

A chameleon can move each of its eyes by itself.

A goat's eyes have pupils that are shaped like rectangles.

What would be a good title for a book that contains these facts?

_____

_____

_____

_____

Use the letters to make words. Try to make one word with all of the letters.

| b | e | h | o | r | r | t |

_____   _____

_____   _____

_____   _____

The lion _____ her prey.

stalking

stalk

stalks

Circle the words that should not be capitalized.

Paper	June	Kevin
Seat	Friday	April
Month	Dr. Paz	Ohio

Say the name of the picture. Write the letters of the beginning sound.

_____

Write the beginning, middle, and end of a story.

Title: _____

_____

_____

_____

| Beginning |
| ↓ |
| Middle |
| ↓ |
| End |

Say the name of each picture. Color the pictures that have the same number of syllables.

  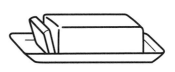

Connect the letters in ABC order. Start at the star.

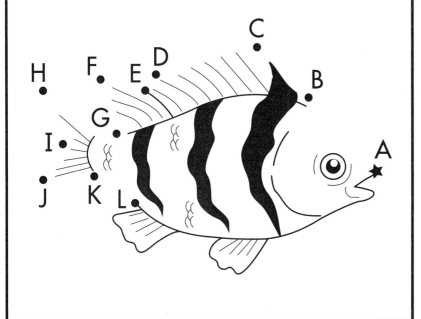

Draw an **X** through the word that does not belong.

carrot   **cake**

peas   **tomato**

Write each sight word in the correct word shape.

fly   give   round

Storms can take all forms. A storm can have lightning and thunder. Some storms have strong winds. A hurricane or a tornado can be dangerous.

The author told me that

_____

_____ .

The picture shows me that

_____ .

Rewrite the sentence to add more detail.

Mom and dad took us to the store.

_____

_____

Write the word one letter at a time.

school

_____

_____ _____

_____ _____ _____

_____ _____ _____ _____

_____ _____ _____ _____ _____

_____ _____ _____ _____ _____ _____

Write a proper noun for the common noun.

song

_____

_____

Trace the words using four colors.

_____

open

open

open

open

Write a sentence that ends with a period. Use the word **before** in the sentence.

_____

_____

_____

_____

Draw a line to match each word to the correct category.

anyone

both   **singular**

many   **plural**

everything

Write a glossary entry for a word that might appear in a book about camping.

_____

_____

_____

_____

_____

Color the verbs.

tight   build

monkey

watch   quit

Draw lines to match the word parts to complete the words.

care   ful

jump   less

hope   ing

Underline the adjectives.

She is dainty as snowdrops that fall
    from the skies,

Is this dear little Kitten with bright,
    shiny eyes

And velvety ears and pretty pink nose

And lovely white suit of soft, furry
    clothes.

How do you think the author feels
about the cat? How do you know?

_____

_____

_____

Color the word that names the picture.

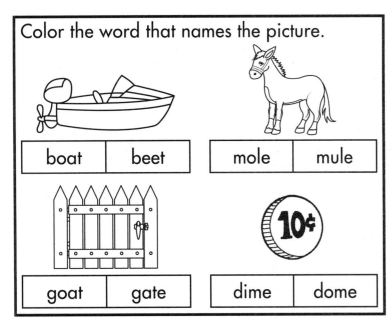

boat	beet

mole	mule

goat	gate

dime	dome

James and Mary _____

about their project during recess.

talk

talks

talking

Say. Connect. Write.

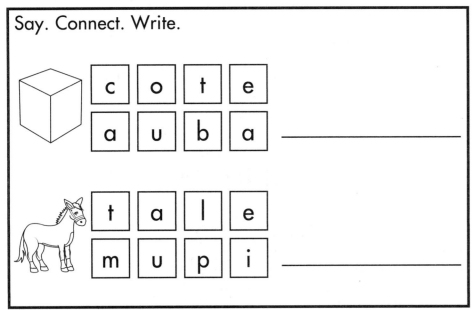

c	o	t	e
a	u	b	a

_____

t	a	l	e
m	u	p	i

_____

Say the name of the picture. Write the letters of the beginning sound.

_____

Write an answer to the question in a complete sentence. Underline the capital letter in your sentence. Circle the ending punctuation.

Do you think that your bedtime is a good time for you to go to sleep? Why or why not?

_____

_____

Rewrite the sentence correctly.

mom put pickles cheese and ketchup on dads sandwich _____

_____

Sort the words.

upset   **gloomy**   **joyful**

merry   **blue**   **cheerful**

Means Happy	Means Sad

Write the letters to spell the word **once**.

o____ce   ____nce

on____e   onc____

Use the word in a sentence.

_____

_____

Say the name of the picture. Choose the correct spelling.

○ **py**

○ **pie**

○ **pye**

Find the singular and plural forms of each word. Color them the same color.

Use the words to write a sentence.

carries	a	hose	firefighter	the	heavy

_____

_____

Find and circle the words. There are two of each one.

has   **live**   **open**

h   t   y   l   h   h   a   s
a   i   h   i   r   i   o   d
s   k   l   v   v   f   p   a
k   o   p   e   n   m   e   f
l   i   v   e   b   l   n   c

Write a proper noun for the common noun.

month

_____

Turn **map** into **son** by changing one letter at a time.

map

m_____p

_____op

to_____

_____on

Today is Mom's birthday! We are having a party. The strawberry cake is ready. Everyone gathers around the table to sing "Happy Birthday." We cut and eat the cake. What a fun party!

Write one more sentence for this story.
Think: What else you would like to know about?

_____

_____

_____

_____

Name _____

Draw a picture for each word.

sharp	**dull**

Say the name of each picture. Write the letters of each word in the boxes.

Unscramble each word. Write the correct spelling. Circle the digraph.

alewh _____

whtea _____

skihw _____

Use the diagram to write at least two sentences about the water cycle.

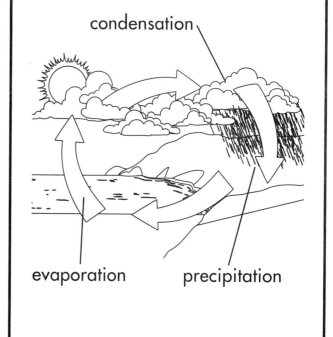

condensation

evaporation   precipitation

_____

_____

_____

_____

Draw lines to divide each word into syllables.

q u i e t

s w e e t e s t

s h o r t e r

Use the letters to make words. Try to make one word with all of the letters.

g	i	m	n	n	o	r

_____   _____

_____   _____

_____   _____

Rover _____ the rope toy

out of my hand!

pull

pulled

pulling

Circle the words that have almost the same meaning.

little	sticky	immense
round	giant	rough
huge	striped	dull

Say the name of the picture. Write the letters of the beginning sound.

_____

Write a report card for a book character. Circle the letter grade for each trait.

A = Excellent   D = Below Average
B = Good   NI = Needs
C = Average   Improvement

Character's Name: _____

Comments: _____

_____

Friendly	A	B	C	D	NI
Caring	A	B	C	D	NI
Honest	A	B	C	D	NI
Problem Solver	A	B	C	D	NI
Clean	A	B	C	D	NI

Say the name of each picture. Color the pictures that have the same number of syllables.

Connect the letters in ABC order. Start at the star.

S T U
R   V
X W
Q
P
O   Y
N   Z
M★

Draw an **X** through the word that does not belong.

fork   **pot**

plate   **napkin**

Write each sight word in the correct word shape.

has   **live**   **open**

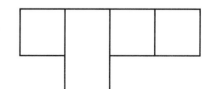

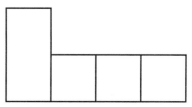

Octopuses are flexible creatures. They do not have bones in their bodies. They can move in all different directions. Some octopuses even make the shape of other animals in order to stay safe.

The author told me that

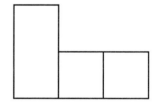

_____

_____ .

The picture shows me that

_____ .

Rewrite the sentence to add more detail.

I am tired after practice.

_____

_____

Write the word one letter at a time.

brother

___

___ ___

___ ___ ___

___ ___ ___ ___

___ ___ ___ ___ ___

___ ___ ___ ___ ___ ___

Write a proper noun for the common noun.

doctor

_____

_____

Trace the words using four colors.

some

some

some

some

Write a sentence that ends with a period. Use the word **during** in the sentence.

_____

_____

_____

_____

Name _____   Week 31, Day 1

Draw a line to match each word to the correct category.

few

each   **singular**

anything   **plural**

many

Draw a picture of something that you might see on a page about vehicles. Add a caption under your drawing.

Color the words that have correct punctuation.

isn't

don't

ca'nt

arent'

won't

Add a prefix or a suffix to each word. Write the number of syllables in the new word.

_____hook_____ ☐

_____view_____ ☐

There was an Old Man with a beard,
Who said, "It is just as I feared!
Two Owls and a Hen, four Larks and a Wren,
Have all built their nests in my beard."

What is the meaning of the word **feared** in this poem?

_____

_____

_____

_____

_____

© Carson-Dellosa • CD-104875   137

Color the word that names the picture.

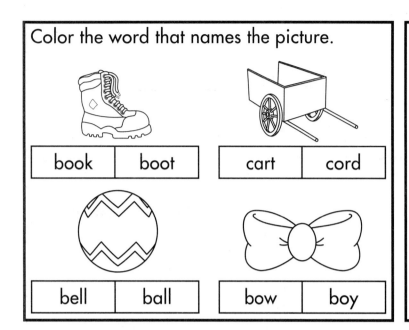

book	boot

cart	cord

bell	ball

bow	boy

The class _____ two songs at the concert tomorrow.

sing

sings

will sing

Say. Connect. Write.

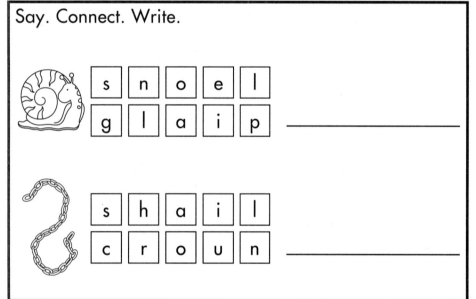

s	n	o	e	l
g	l	a	i	p

_____

s	h	a	i	l
c	r	o	u	n

_____

Say the name of the picture. Write the letters of the ending sound.

_____

Write an answer to the question in a complete sentence. Underline the capital letter in your sentence. Circle the ending punctuation.

What is your favorite part of a party? Why?

_____

_____

Rewrite the sentence correctly.

i took sids dog for a walk fed it dinner and brushed its fur _____

_____

Sort the words.

great   **lousy**

awful   **wonderful**

Means Good	Means Bad

Say the name of the picture. Choose the correct spelling.

○ **bred**

○ **breed**

○ **bread**

Write the letters to spell the word **after**.

a___ter   aft___r

af___er   ___fter

Use the word in a sentence.

_____

_____

Find the singular and plural forms of each word. Color them the same color.

leaf

chef

loaf

knives

leaves

loaves

chefs

knife

Use the words to write a sentence.

at	fast	bird	look	that	fly

_____

_____

Find and circle the words. There are two of each one.

giving   **once**   **thank**

t	p	t	y	j	l	o	b	o
h	i	g	i	v	i	n	g	n
a	a	k	l	d	u	c	d	c
n	t	h	a	n	k	e	w	e
k	j	s	g	i	v	i	n	g

Write a proper noun for the common noun.

state

_____

_____

Turn **pig** into **box** by changing one letter at a time.

pig

pi_____

_____in

bi_____

b_____b

bo_____

A small dinosaur walked across the rocky land. It looked for some green plants to eat, but it did not find any. It looked for some water to drink, but it did not find any. A loud noise scared the dinosaur. It ran quickly into the woods to hide. The dinosaur waited and looked around. There in front of him was a stream and some yummy plants to eat.

What do you think made the loud noise?

_____

Write an ending to this story.

_____

_____

Draw a picture for each word.

easy	**difficult**

Say the name of each picture. Write the letters of each word in the boxes.

Unscramble each word. Write the correct spelling. Circle the digraph.

ngik _____

ignth _____

spirgn _____

Before they were leaders, some US presidents had different jobs.

Abraham Lincoln	lawyer
Andrew Johnson	tailor
Harry Truman	hat and clothing salesman
Jimmy Carter	peanut farmer
Ronald Reagan	movie actor

Write a title for this chart.

_____

Which two presidents had jobs working with clothes?

_____

_____

Write the base words.

bravest _____

larger _____

giving _____

Use the letters to make words. Try to make one word with all of the letters.

c	d	e	h	i	l	n	r

_____   _____

_____   _____

_____   _____

Matt _____ three buckets

of blueberries yesterday.

will pick

picked

picking

Circle the words that have almost the same meaning.

funny	slow	awful
smart	easy	cool
swift	fast	quick

Say the name of the picture. Write the letters of the ending sound.

_____

Compare two characters in different stories. Write at least four traits in the diagram.

_____   _____

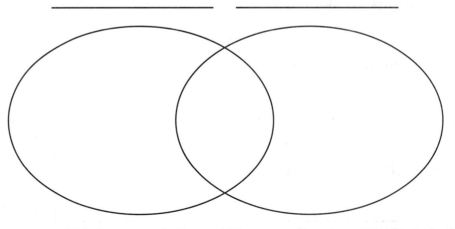

Say the name of each picture. Color the pictures that have the same number of syllables.

Connect the letters in ABC order. Start at the star.

Draw an **X** through the word that does not belong.

foot   **add**

equals   **minus**

Write each sight word in the correct word shape.

give   once   thank

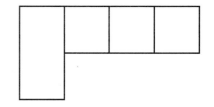

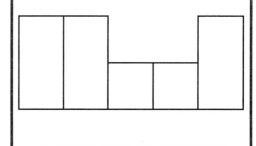

Baseball is an old sport. It was being played in the 1800s in the United States. Two teams take turns at bat and out in the field. There are nine players on each team. Players try to get runs to win points for their teams.

The author told me that

_____.

The picture shows me that

_____.

Rewrite the sentence to add more detail.

William put on his socks and shoes.

_____

_____

Write the word one letter at a time.

window

____

____ ____

____ ____ ____

____ ____ ____ ____

____ ____ ____ ____ ____

____ ____ ____ ____ ____ ____

Write a proper noun for the common noun.

character

_____

_____

Trace the words using four colors.

when

when

when

when

Write a sentence that ends with an exclamation point. Use the word **behind** in the sentence.

_____

_____

_____

_____

_____

Draw a line to match each verb to its tense.

drives

past

jumped

present

will call

future

laughed

Write a topic sentence for a paragraph about germs.

_____

_____

_____

_____

_____

Color the words that have correct punctuation.

she'll

youl'l

they'll

I'll

w'ell

When I was down beside the sea
A wooden spade they gave to me
To dig the sandy shore.
My holes were empty like a cup,
In every hole the sea came up,
Till it could come no more.

To what does the child compare his holes?

_____

_____

_____

_____

_____

Add a prefix or a suffix to each word. Write the number of syllables in the new word.

_____drink_____ ☐

_____clean_____ ☐

Name _____ **Week 33, Day 2**

Color the word that names the picture.

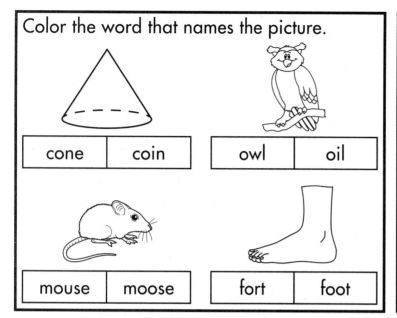

cone	coin
owl	oil
mouse	moose
fort	foot

Wolves _____ in packs.

travels

traveling

travel

Say. Connect. Write.

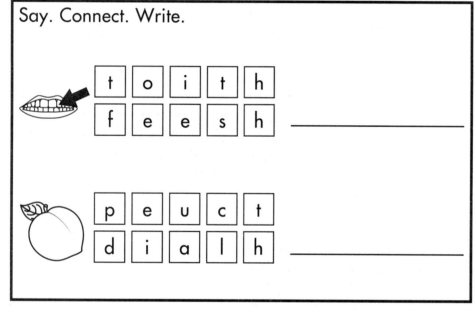

| t | o | i | t | h |
| f | e | e | s | h | _____

| p | e | u | c | t |
| d | i | a | l | h | _____

Say the name of the picture. Write the letters of the ending sound.

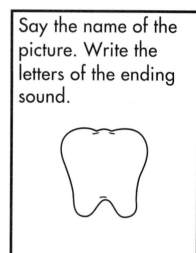

_____

Write an answer to the question in a complete sentence. Underline the capital letter in your sentence. Circle the ending punctuation.

When was the last time you were proud of yourself? Why?

_____

_____

Rewrite the sentence correctly.

a cat sniffs at it's food carefully to make sure its fresh _____

_____

Sort the words.

huge   **small**

large   **tiny**

Means Big	Means Little

Write the letters to spell the word **thank**.

_____hank   th_____nk

tha_____k   t_____ank

Use the word in a sentence.

_____

_____

Say the name of the picture.
Choose the correct spelling.

○ **tertel**

○ **turtle**

○ **tirtle**

Find the singular and plural
forms of each word. Color
them the same color.

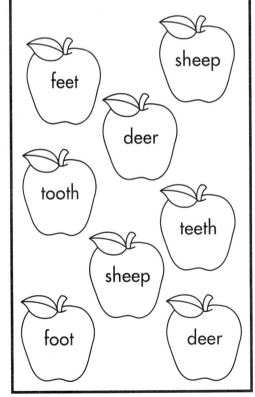

feet, sheep, deer, tooth, teeth, sheep, foot, deer

Name _____

Name _____

Use the words to write a sentence.

before	I	dinner	to	eat	want	dessert

_____

_____

Fill the grid with the sight words by writing one letter in each box. Fill the empty boxes with random letters. Then, circle the sight words in the puzzle.

as   by   could   fly   put   just

Write a proper noun for the common noun.

book

_____

_____

Turn **path** into **fish** by changing one letter at a time.

path

_____ath

ba_____h

_____ash

d_____sh

_____ish

The girl put on her jacket and helmet. She grabbed her bag and gear. As soon as she buckled her seat belt, she was off! As she flew into space, she saw the moon. The moon looked gray and bumpy.

Where is the girl?

_____

What words were a clue?

_____

_____

Draw a picture for each word.

strong	**weak**

Say the name of each picture. Write the letters of each word in the boxes.

Unscramble each **long e** word. Write the correct spelling.

thtee   _____

ceahb   _____

lshea   _____

Use the diagram to answer the questions.

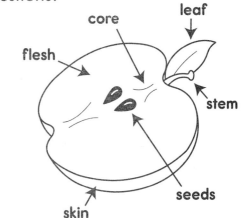

What does this diagram show?

_____

_____

Which parts of the apple could you eat?

_____

_____

Draw lines to divide each word into syllables.

t a l k i n g

f a s t e r

p r e s c h o o l

Use the letters to make words. Try to make one word with all of the letters.

a	b	d	h	i	r	t	y

_____   _____

_____   _____

_____   _____

Dolphins _____ to each other with many different sounds.

will talk

talks

talk

Circle the words that have a prefix.

preview	hopeless	teacher
careful	unlike	exciting
quickly	biggest	rewind

Say the name of the picture. Write the letters of the ending sound.

_____

Compare two characters in the same story. Write at least four traits in the diagram.

_____   _____

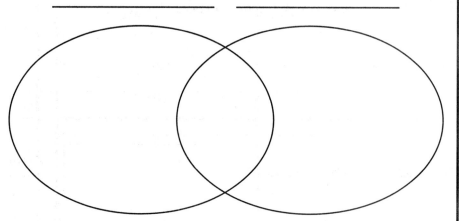

Say the name of each picture. Color the pictures that have the same number of syllables.

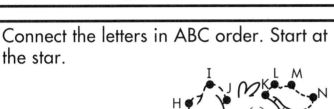

Connect the letters in ABC order. Start at the star.

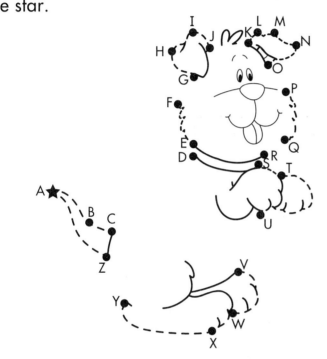

Draw an **X** through the word that does not belong.

dance   **swim**

talk   **run**

Write each word in the correct word shape.

red   orange   yellow

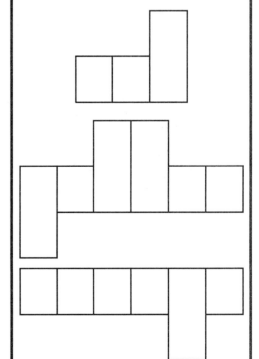

Some birds eat worms and bugs. Some birds eat seeds or berries. Other birds eat small rodents, fish, or even other birds. The shape of a bird's beak can tell you what a bird might eat. Different shaped beaks have different purposes.

The author told me that

_____.

The picture shows me that

_____.

Rewrite the sentence to add more detail.

She said that the car was moving fast.

_____

_____

Write the word one letter at a time.

ground

_____

_____ _____

_____ _____ _____

_____ _____ _____ _____

_____ _____ _____ _____ _____

_____ _____ _____ _____ _____ _____

Write a proper noun for the common noun.

team

_____

_____

Trace the words using four colors.

once

once

once

once

Write a sentence that ends with a period. Use the word **around** in the sentence.

_____

_____

_____

_____

_____

Draw a line to match each verb to its tense.

slobbered

                past

sleeps

                present

will eat

                future

cries

Draw a chart that might show a class schedule for a Monday.

_____

_____

_____

_____

_____

Color the words that have correct punctuation.

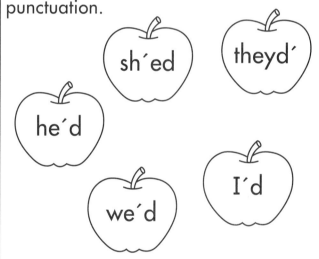

sh´ed

theyd´

he´d

we´d

I´d

Once I saw a little bird
Come hop, hop, hop;
So I cried, "Little bird,
Will you stop, stop, stop?"

I was going to the window
To say, "How do you do?"
But he shook his little tail,
And far away he flew.

Why do you think the author repeats the word **hop** in the second line of the poem?

_____

_____

_____

_____

Add a prefix or a suffix to each word. Write the number of syllables in the new word.

_____help_____

_____read_____

Color the word that names the picture.

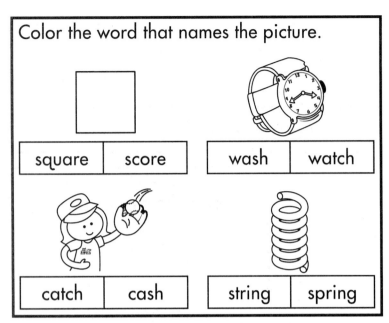

square	score
wash	watch
catch	cash
string	spring

You should _____ your

shoelace before you trip.

tie

ties

tied

Say. Connect. Write.

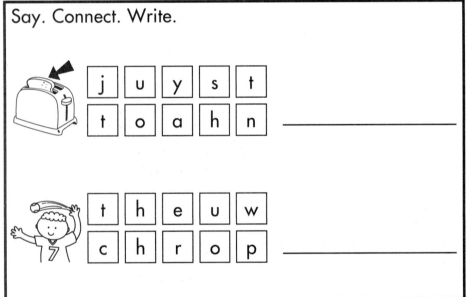

| j | u | y | s | t |
| t | o | a | h | n | _____

| t | h | e | u | w |
| c | h | r | o | p | _____

Say the name of the picture. Write the letters of the ending sound.

_____

Write an answer to the question in a complete sentence. Underline the capital letter in your sentence. Circle the ending punctuation.

What is your favorite season? Why?

_____

_____

Rewrite the sentence correctly.

why did the golfer where too pears of pants _____

_____

Just in case he got a hole-in-one!

Sort the words.

glance   **march**

stroll   **watch**

Means Walk	Means Look

Write the letters to spell the word **every**.

____very   ev___ry

e___ery   eve___y

Use the word in a sentence.

_____

_____

Say the name of the picture. Choose the correct spelling.

○ **klowd**

○ **clowd**

○ **cloud**

Find the singular and plural forms of each word. Color them the same color.

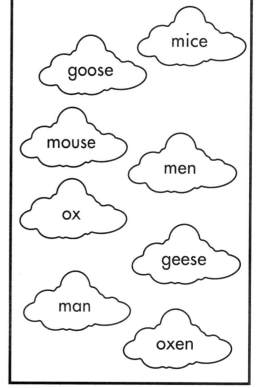

mice
goose
mouse
men
ox
geese
man
oxen

Use the words to write a sentence.

| angry | stairs | stomped | the | up | child | the |

_____

_____

Fill the grid with the sight words by writing one letter in each box. Fill the empty boxes with random letters. Then, circle the sight words in the puzzle.

an   **him**   **know**   **of**   **open**   **some**

Write a proper noun for the common noun.

pet

_____

Turn **read** into **goat** by changing one letter at a time.

read

_____ead

bea_____

b_____at

_____oat

Rabbit eats fresh carrots from the garden. One morning, there were no more carrots. "Where did all the carrots go?" asked Rabbit. Later that day, her friend Deer passed by with a carrot. Rabbit was hungry and mad. Deer stopped to share the carrot with Rabbit. They ate and laughed together.

What do you think happened to all of Rabbit's carrots?

_____

What is one word that describes Deer at the end of the story?

_____

Draw a picture for each word.

useful	**useless**

Say the name of each picture. Write the letters of each word in the boxes.

Unscramble each **long a** word. Write the correct spelling.

ainpt _____

rspya _____

kstea _____

Use the diagram to answer the questions.

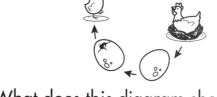

What does this diagram show?

_____

_____

What is one thing you can learn from this diagram?

_____

_____

_____

Separate the prefix or suffix from each word.

review _____ _____

turning _____ _____

smallest _____ _____

Use the letters to make words. Try to make one word with all of the letters.

c	e	i	p	r	t	u

_____   _____

_____   _____

_____

Earth _____ on its axis

while it orbits the sun.

rotates

rotating

rotate

Circle the words that have a suffix.

misspell	dislike	fearless
return	defrost	baker
undo	recycle	careful

Say the name of the picture. Write the letters of the beginning sound.

_____

Complete the diagram with details from a story you just read.

Cause

Effect

Say the name of each picture. Color the pictures that have the same number of syllables.

bud: a new, unformed flower, leaf, or branch

nectar: a sweet liquid inside flowers that some animals, birds, and insects drink

pollen: a powder that plants make and insects help move from plant to plant

seed: a hard shell with a young plant inside

This glossary is probably from a book about _____.

animals   juice   plants

The words in a glossary are placed in _____ order.

counting   alphabetical   word-length

Draw an **X** through the word that does not belong.

pillow   robe

sheet   blanket

Write each word in the correct word shape.

green   blue   purple

It can get really hot in a desert. Many living things make their homes there. These plants and animals have traits that help them live in dry, hot areas.

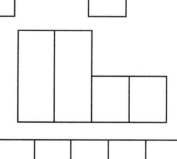

The author told me that

_____.

The picture shows me that

_____.

Rewrite the sentence to add more detail.

We went on vacation and stayed in a hotel.

_____

_____

Write the word one letter at a time.

picture

____

____ ____

____ ____ ____

____ ____ ____ ____

____ ____ ____ ____ ____

____ ____ ____ ____ ____ ____

____ ____ ____ ____ ____ ____ ____

Write a proper noun for the common noun.

restaurant

_____

_____

Trace the words using four colors.

_____

every

every

every

every

Write a sentence that ends with a question mark. Use the word **outside** in the sentence.

_____

_____

_____

_____

Draw a line to match each verb to its tense.

will jump

       past

stare

       present

will write

       future

chased

Write a glossary entry for a word that might appear in a book about birds.

_____

_____

_____

_____

_____

Color the words that have correct punctuation.

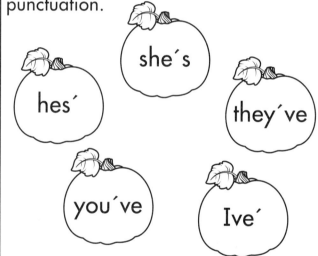

hes´   she´s   they´ve   you´ve   Ive´

Add a prefix or a suffix to each word. Write the number of syllables in the new word.

_____heat_____   ☐

_____act_____   ☐

In winter I get up at night,
And dress by yellow candle light.
In summer quite the other way,
I have to go to bed by day.
I have to go to bed and see
The birds still hopping on the tree,
Or hear the grown-up people´s feet,
Still going past me in the street.
And does it not seem hard to you,
When all the sky is clear and blue,
And I should like so much to play,
To have to go to bed by day?

Give two reasons why the child does not like to go to bed in summer.

_____

_____

_____

_____

Color the word that names the picture.

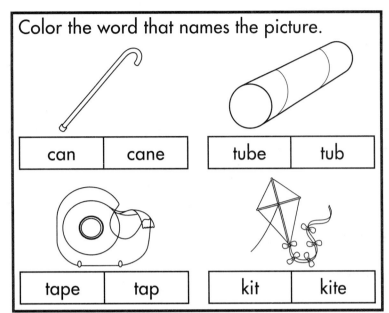

can	cane

tube	tub

tape	tap

kit	kite

The team _____ where to eat dinner next Friday.

decide

deciding

will decide

Say. Connect. Write.

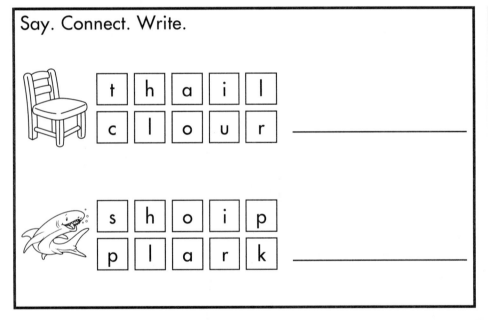

t	h	a	i	l
c	l	o	u	r

_____

s	h	o	i	p
p	l	a	r	k

_____

Say the name of the picture. Write the letters of the ending sound.

_____

Write an answer to the question in a complete sentence. Underline the capital letter in your sentence. Circle the ending punctuation.

If you could eat only one color of food for an entire week, what color would it be? Why?

_____

_____

Rewrite the sentence correctly.

a tornadoe can strip bark from trees and pluck fethers from chikens _____

_____

Sort the words.

giggle	**exclaim**
chuckle	**shout**

Means Laugh	Means Say

Say the name of the picture.
Choose the correct spelling.

○ **camle**

○ **kamel**

○ **camel**

Write the letters to spell the word **again**.

aga____n   ag____in

____gain   a____ain

Use the word in a sentence.

_____

_____

Find the singular and plural
forms of each word. Color
them the same color.

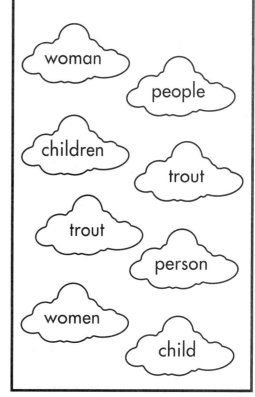

woman

people

children

trout

trout

person

women

child

163

Use the words to write a sentence.

| my | do | lesson | to | when | piano | go | I |

_____

_____

Fill the grid with the sight words by writing one letter in each box. Fill the empty boxes with random letters. Then, circle the sight words in the puzzle.

after   ask   every   give   has   take

Write a proper noun for the common noun.

game

_____

Turn **stop** into **trip** by changing one letter at a time.

stop

s_____op

_____lop

p_____op

_____rop

dr_____p

_____rip

Tomorrow the class is going on a field trip to the museum. The teacher will wear a red shirt and the students will wear yellow shirts. All of the students need to bring a lunch and a drink. The bus will leave the school at eight o'clock and return to school at three o'clock. Everyone is **eager** to go on the trip.

What do the students need to do to get ready for the field trip?

_____

What does **eager** mean in the last sentence?

_____

Name _____

Name _____

Draw a picture for each word.

simple	fancy

Say the name of each picture. Write the letters of each word in the boxes.

Unscramble each **/au/** word. Write the correct spelling.

asmll _____

wlacr _____

cesau _____

Draw lines to divide each word into its syllables.

f r i e n d l y

w r o n g l y

k i n d n e s s

A sea turtle **migrates** to the same beach where she was born. She will lay her eggs here. First, she drags herself up onto the beach. Then, she uses her flippers to scoop out sand to make a hole for her eggs. Next, the sea turtle covers the eggs with sand. Finally, she moves back to the water as fast as she can. Her eggs will hatch in about two months. The baby sea turtles will make their way to the ocean where they will grow to adults. The females will come back to the same beach to lay their eggs when they are ready.

A sea turtle lays eggs every two to three years in late spring and summer. A sea turtle will lay about 100 eggs. The eggs look like small white balls.

What is the meaning of the bold word in the passage?

sleeps   **travels**   **eats**

© Carson-Dellosa • CD-104875

Use the letters to make words. Try to make one word with all of the letters. (Hint: Some people eat turkey on this holiday.)

a	g	g	h	i	i
k	n	n	T	s	v

_____

_____   _____

A raccoon _____ its food

before eating it.

will wash

washing

wash

Circle the words that have the same root word.

disappear	helper	running
likely	unlike	likeness
helpful	mistrust	replay

Say the name of the picture. Write the letters of the beginning sound.

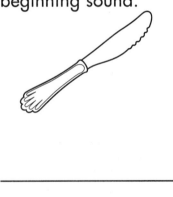

_____

Write at least two problems and solutions from a story you have read.

Title: _____

Problems	Solutions

Say the name of each picture. Color the pictures that have the same number of syllables.

Connect the letters in ABC order. Start at the star.

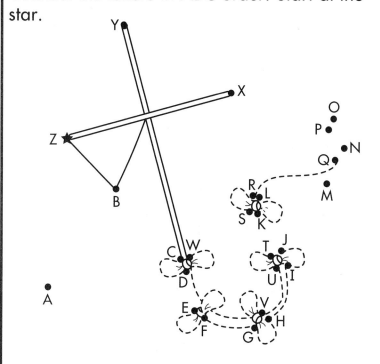

Draw an **X** through the word that does not belong.

furry   **scratchy**

fluffy   **soft**

Write each sight word in the correct word shape.

brown   black   gray

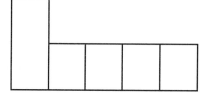

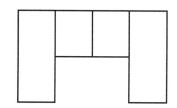

Look at the picture. Think about what book you might see the picture in. Write at least one sentence that might be written on the same page.

_____

_____

_____

_____

Rewrite the sentence to add more detail.

The man climbed up and got the kitten out of the tree.

_____

_____

Write the word one letter at a time.

children

____

____ ____

____ ____ ____

____ ____ ____ ____

____ ____ ____ ____ ____

____ ____ ____ ____ ____ ____

____ ____ ____ ____ ____ ____ ____ ____

Write a proper noun for the common noun.

car

_____

Trace the words using four colors.

_____

again

again

again

again

Write a sentence that ends with an exclamation point. Use the word **across** in the sentence.

_____

_____

_____

_____

Draw a line to match each verb to its tense.

blinks

past

shouted

present

gobbles

future

will ask

Write a topic sentence for a paragraph about ice cream.

_____

_____

_____

_____

_____

Color the words that have correct punctuation.

your'e

she's

I'm

we're

hes'

Brown and furry
Caterpillar in a hurry,
Take your walk
To the shady leaf, or stalk,
Or what not,
Which may be the chosen spot.
No toad spy you,
Hovering bird of prey pass by you;
Spin and die,
To live again a butterfly.

What is this poem about?

_____

_____

_____

_____

Add a prefix or a suffix to each word. Write the number of syllables in the new word.

_____joy_____   [ ]

_____fear_____   [ ]

Color the word that names the picture.

paws	pose

clown	claw

cone	coin

news	nose

The kicker _____ the ball for the winning point.

punting

will punt

punted

Say. Connect. Write.

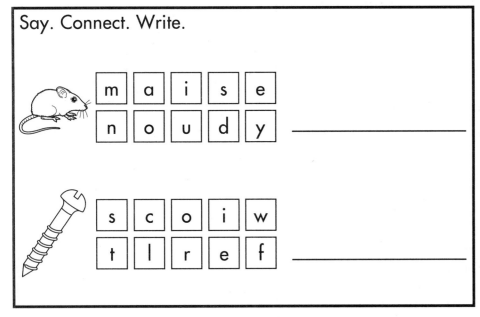

m	a	i	s	e
n	o	u	d	y

_____

s	c	o	i	w
t	l	r	e	f

_____

Say the name of the picture. Write the letters of the ending sound.

_____

Write an answer to the question in a complete sentence. Underline the capital letter in your sentence. Circle the ending punctuation.

Imagine your family has decided to move to a different country. How do you feel about it? Why?

_____

_____

Rewrite the sentence correctly.

what is at the end of everything _____

_____

The letter **g**.

Sort the words.

nap   **gobble**

feast   **doze**

Means Eat	Means Sleep

Say the name of the picture.
Choose the correct spelling.

○ **knief**

○ **knife**

○ **knyf**

Find the singular and plural
forms of each word. Color
them the same color.

pants

scissors

cactus

pants

cacti

dice

scissors

die

Write the letters to spell the word **could**.

co____ld   ____ould

c____uld   cou____d

Use the word in a sentence.

_____

_____

Use the words to write a sentence.

| to | but | want | it | to | go | raining | I | park | is | the |

_____

_____

Fill the grid with the sight words by writing one letter in each box. Fill the empty boxes with random letters. Then, circle the sight words in the puzzle.

again   **let**   **live**   **thank**   **them**   **when**

Write a proper noun for the common noun.

president

_____

Turn **clock** into **stack** by changing one letter at a time.

clock

cl_____ck

_____lick

s_____ick

st_____ck

Eve walked to her new classroom. She looked all around but did not see her friend Ben anywhere. She found a yellow chair and her name on the desk. The teacher came over to talk to her. Eve thought that Ben must be in another class. She sat and wondered who her new friends would be this year.

What do you think the teacher said to Eve?

_____

How do you think Eve feels when she does not see her friend Ben?

_____

Draw a picture for each word.

| **borrow** | **return** |
| | |

Say the name of each picture. Write the letters of each word in the boxes.

Unscramble each **/ou/** word. Write the correct spelling.

owcnr   _____

lewto   _____

oucbne   _____

Separate the prefix or suffix from each word.

boxes   _____ _____

redo   _____ _____

higher   _____ _____

Play Dough

Ingredients:
2 cups flour
4 tablespoons cream of tartar
2 tablespoons cooking oil
1 cup salt
2 cups boiling water
glitter (optional)
food coloring (optional)

Directions:
1. Put all of the ingredients in a bowl and mix.
2. Once the dough has come together, dump it on a flat surface and knead it until it is smooth.
3. Put the dough in an airtight container until you are ready to play with it.

What does the word **optional** mean as used after the last two ingredients?

_____

Name _____

Use the letters to make words. Try to make one word with all of the letters.
(Hint: You can use this to keep your teeth clean and healthy.)

o	r	h	h	t
b	u	s	o	t

_____   _____

_____

Dave _____ 60 words per minute.

type

types

typing

Circle the words that have the same root word.

replay	playing	playful
disagree	mistake	hopeful
smallest	return	preview

Say the name of the picture. Write the letters of the ending sound.

_____

Complete the diagram with details from a nonfiction book you have read.

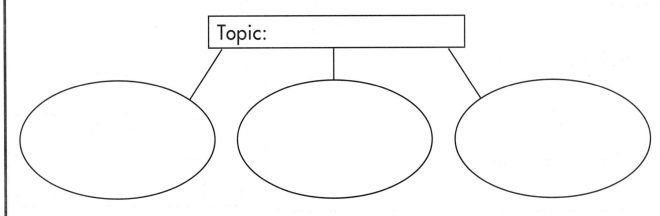

Topic:

Name _____

Say the name of each picture. Color the pictures that have the same number of syllables.

   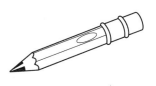

Connect the letters in ABC order. Start at the star.

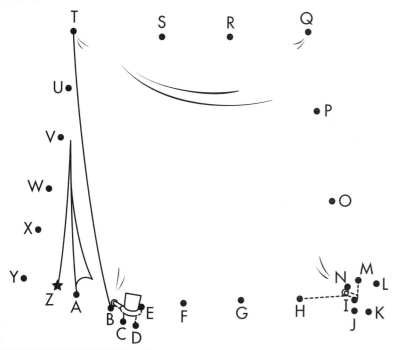

Draw an **X** through the word that does not belong.

slow   **drive**

bake   **run**

Write each sight word in the correct word shape.

pink   **violet**   **white**

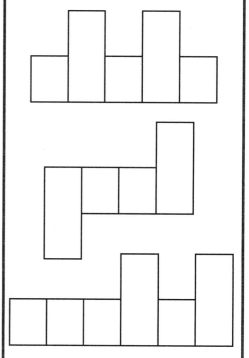

There are many winter sports. Skating and hockey are done on ice. Skiing and snowboarding are done on snowy mountains. It is important to have the right gear to stay safe and warm.

The author told me that

_____.

The picture shows me that

_____.

Rewrite the sentence to add more detail.

Eat your dinner and you can have dessert.

_____

_____

Write the word one letter at a time.

birthday

___

___ ___

___ ___ ___

___ ___ ___ ___

___ ___ ___ ___ ___

___ ___ ___ ___ ___ ___

___ ___ ___ ___ ___ ___ ___

Write a proper noun for the common noun.

author

_____

Trace the words using four colors.

could

could

could

could

Write a sentence that ends with a period. Use the word **through** in the sentence.

_____

_____

_____

_____

_____

an	been	could	find
again	ask	come	every
after	as	by	each
about	any	but	down

give	from	fly	first
him	her	has	had
know	just	into	how
more	may	live	let

old	over	ran	saw
of	open	put	said
now	one	please	run
no	once	part	red

small	than	them	very
she	soon	the	up
see	some	that	this
say	so	thank	they

Answer Key

Day 1

Day 2

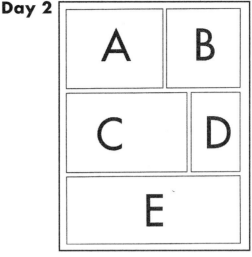

Day 3

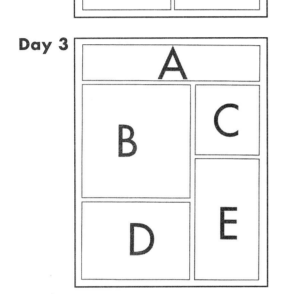

Day 4

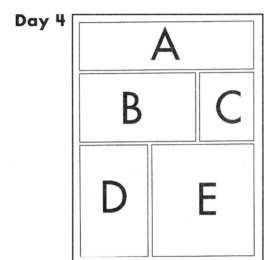

Week 1, Day 1 (page 17)
A. Students should draw a child with an umbrella or wearing rain gear. B. Check students' matching. C. dog, boy, house; D. 1, 1, 1; E. cat, car, comb, cow, can

Week 1, Day 2 (page 18)
A. hat, pig, bed, mop; B. jumps; C. bag, pan; D. Check students' tracing. E. Answers will vary.

Week 1, Day 3 (page 19)
A. Mrs. Brown is my teacher. B. Colors: blue, red, white; Numbers: one, six, three; C. cup; D. y, n, a; Answers will vary. E. Check students' coloring.

Week 1, Day 4 (page 20)
A. The hen sat. B. Check students' circling. C. pot; D. bat, cat, sat; Answers will vary. E. black, They play.

Week 2, Day 1 (page 21)
A. swims: shark, whale, fish, dolphin; flies: owl, bee, eagle; B. Down: bag, Across: cat; C. map, cab, hat; D. star/fish, pop/corn, back/pack; E. from top to bottom, left to right: body, wheel, frame

Week 2, Day 2 (page 22)
A. Answers will vary. Letters should make the word *rain*. B. sits; C. cap, tap, map; D. Check students' tracing. E. Answers will vary.

Answer Key

Week 2, Day 3 (page 23)
A. cap, bag; B. Check students' drawing.
C. ant; D. Answers will vary. E. saw,
with, came

Week 2, Day 4 (page 24)
A. Answers will vary. B. Check students'
spelling. C. pig; D. Check students' tracing.
E. Answers will vary.

Week 3, Day 1 (page 25)
A. a star; B. Check students' matching.
C. bed, cat, girl; D. 1, 1, 1; E. Check
students' coloring to see an uppercase *A*.

Week 3, Day 2 (page 26)
A. rug, bat, fan, fox; B. barks; C. cat, fan;
D. Check students' tracing. E. Answers
will vary.

Week 3, Day 3 (page 27)
A. Wild pandas are found only in China.
B. Colors: black, orange, yellow; Numbers:
four, nine, two; C. bed; D. l, d, o; Answers
will vary. E. Check students' coloring.

Week 3, Day 4 (page 28)
A. The dog ran. B. Check students' circling.
C. hat; D. Answers will vary. E. blue, in
the park

Week 4, Day 1 (page 29)
A. red: cherry, heart, strawberry; green:
plant, grasshopper, pear; B. Across: pen;
Down: net; C. hen, ten, bed; D. ant/hill,
base/ball, bath/tub; E. He makes the bed.
He mops on days 2 and 5.

Week 4, Day 2 (page 30)
A. Answers will vary. Letters should make the
word *name*, *mane*, or *mean*. B. roll;
C. jam, ham, yam; D. Check students'
tracing. E. Answers will vary.

Week 4, Day 3 (page 31)
A. box, mop; B. Check students' drawing.
C. bat; D. Answers will vary. E. want,
new, have

Week 4, Day 4 (page 32)
A. Answers will vary. B. Check students'
spelling. C. box; D. Check students' tracing.
E. Answers will vary.

Week 5, Day 1 (page 33)
A. The clock struck one. B. Check students'
matching. C. log, apple, mom; D. 1, 1, 1;
E. pen, pan, pig, pie, pin, plant

Week 5, Day 2 (page 34)
A. pot, cup, pen, net; B. play; C. tag, hat;
D. Check students' tracing. E. Answers will
vary.

Week 5, Day 3 (page 35)
A. I was born on the fourth of April.
B. Colors: brown, green, pink; Numbers:
five, one, two; C. pin; D. k, s, a; Answers will
vary. E. Check students' coloring.

Week 5, Day 4 (page 36)
A. Tom plays ball. B. Check students'
circling. C. bird; D. Answers will vary.
E. happy, nap

Week 6, Day 1 (page 37)
A. kitchen: fork, stove, plate; bathroom:
toothbrush, bathtub, hairbrush; B. Across:
fin; Down: wig; C. wig, pin, dip; D. box/car,
fish/bowl, po/lice; E. From left to right and
top to bottom: toy box, chair, rug, door, bed

Answer Key

Week 6, Day 2 (page 38)
A. Answers will vary. Letters should make the word *snow*. B. will grow; C. tab, cab, jab; D. Check students' tracing. Answers will vary.

Week 6, Day 3 (page 39)
A. map, bag; B. Check students´ drawing. C. five; D. Answers will vary. E. of, had, her

Week 6, Day 4 (page 40)
A. Answers will vary. B. Check students´ spelling. C. fan; D. Check students' tracing. E. Answers will vary.

Week 7, Day 1 (page 41)
A. The master, the dame, and the little boy will get a bag. B. Check students' matching. C. egg, dad, school; D. 2, 1, 2; E. Check students' coloring to see an uppercase *E*.

Week 7, Day 2 (page 42)
A. cub, pin, log, pan; B. hop; C. bed, hen; D. Check students' tracing. E. Answers will vary.

Week 7, Day 3 (page 43)
A. The ocean is home to fish, turtles, and whales. B. Inside: rug, fork, bed; Outside: tree, ant, cloud; C. pot; D. a, e, k, t; Answerss will vary. E. Check students´ coloring.

Week 7, Day 4 (page 44)
A. Here is the sled. or, The sled is here. B. Check students' circling. C. ring; D. Answers will vary. E. the leaf, Answers will vary.

Week 8, Day 1 (page 45)
A. Answers will vary. B. Across: log; Down: mop; C. fog, top/pot, hot; D. pig/pen, sea/shore, pan/cake; E. trains A and D; at a train station

Week 8, Day 2 (page 46)
A. Answers will vary. Letters should make the word *table*. B. make; C. bed, red, fed; D. Check students' tracing. E. Answers will vary.

Week 8, Day 3 (page 47)
A. crib, knit; B. Answers will vary. C. cup; D. Answers will vary. E. some, his, as

Week 8, Day 4 (page 48)
A. Answers will vary. B. Check students´ spelling. C. cow; D. Check students´ tracing. E. Answers will vary.

Week 9, Day 1 (page 49)
A. Answers will vary. B. Check students´ matching. C. pear, baby, car; D. 1, 2, 2; E. leg, lips, lion, lock, leaf

Week 9, Day 2 (page 50)
A. map, bib, sun, rat; B. skates; C. jet, ten; D. Check students' tracing. E. Answers will vary.

Week 9, Day 3 (page 51)
A. Jane rides around the park, but Jed runs around the park. B. Objects: pin, book, hat; People: boy, mom, baby; C. mug; D. h, n, t, e; Answers will vary. E. Check students´ coloring.

Answer Key

Week 9, Day 4 (page 52)
A. I ate the apple. B. Check students´
circling. C. bike; D. Answers will vary.
E. hot, swim

Week 10, Day 1 (page 53)
A. Answers will vary. B. Across: rug; Down:
hut; C. bus/sub, cut, mug/gum; D. rain/
coat, suit/case, air/port; E. Check students´
coloring.

Week 10, Day 2 (page 54)
A. Answers will vary. Letters should make the
word *water*. B. clean; C. pen, ten, hen;
D. Check students' tracing. E. Answers
will vary.

Week 10, Day 3 (page 55)
A. tent, shell; B. Check students' drawing.
C. bee; D. Answers will vary. E. could,
then, him

Week 10, Day 4 (page 56)
A. Answers will vary. B. Check students´
spelling. C. house; D. Check students'
tracing. E. Answers will vary.

Week 11, Day 1 (page 57)
A. character: Goldilocks, Papa Bear; cetting:
house, woods; B. air, food, needs, space,
water; C. sock, park, teacher; D. 2, 1, 2;
E. Check students' coloring to see an
uppercase *I*.

Week 11, Day 2 (page 58)
A. jam, leg, wig, tag; B. paints; C. bib, wig;
D. Check students' tracing. E. Answers will
vary.

Week 11, Day 3 (page 59)
A. Yesterday was hot, but today is hotter.
B. Places: park, home, school; Objects: glue,
ring, car; C. bat; D. e, e, v, r; Answers will
vary. E. Check students' coloring.

Week 11, Day 4 (page 60)
A. That is a big hat. B. Check students´
circling. C. Katie; D. burn, barn;
E. a fish, swims

Week 12, Day 1 (page 61)
A. Answers will vary. B. Across: mask; Down:
lamp; C. cake, gate, cane; D. but/ter, sum/
mer, rab/bit; E. Students should draw a
green and yellow basket (with a written letter
in or out of the basket).

Week 12, Day 2 (page 62)
A. Answers will vary. Letters should make the
word *beard* or *bread*; B. tells; C. dip, lip, tip;
D. Check students' tracing. E. Answers will vary
but drawings should show order.

Week 12, Day 3 (page 63)
A. corn, fork; B. Check students' drawing.
C. rug; D. Answers will vary. E. over, ask,
when

Week 12, Day 4 (page 64)
A. Answers will vary. B. Check students´
spelling. C. Sam; D. Check students' tracing.
E. Answers will vary.

Week 13, Day 1 (page 65)
A. character: Gingerbread boy, fox; setting:
town, river; B. flower, leaf, plant, root, stem;
C. yellow, smooth, loud; D. 1, 2, 2; E. Both a
star and a diamond twinkle.

Answer Key

Week 13, Day 2 (page 66)
A. bug, fan, lip, pin; B. visit; C. pin, lip;
D. Check students' tracing. E. Answers will vary.

Week 13, Day 3 (page 67)
A. What is brown and sticky? B. Nouns: cake, nail, spider; Verbs: jump, run, talk; C. cake; D. r, f, m, o; Answers will vary. E. Check students' coloring.

Week 13, Day 4 (page 68)
A. We see the car. B. Check students' circling. C. Mr. Lee; D. Answers will vary. E. couch, Grandma

Week 14, Day 1 (page 69)
A. Answers will vary. B. Across: tent; Down: bell; C. hive, kite, bike; D. yel/low, wal/let, zip/per; E. clockwise: wing, leg, head

Week 14, Day 2 (page 70)
A. Answers will vary. Letters should make the word *shore* or *horse*; B. watched; C. pin, fin, win; D. Check students' tracing. E. Answers will vary but drawings should show order.

Week 14, Day 3 (page 71)
A. bird, shirt; B. Check students' drawing. C. owl; D. Answers will vary. E. them, were, an

Week 14, Day 4 (page 72)
A. Answers will vary. B. Check students' spelling. C. Dr. Gold; D. Check students' tracing. E. Answers will vary.

Week 15, Day 1 (page 73)
A. Character: wolf, pig; Setting: brick house, straw house; B. egg, frog, gill, hop, lung; C. orange, two, cold; D. 2, 1, 1; E. Check students' coloring to see an uppercase *O*.

Week 15, Day 2 (page 74)
A. bag, ham, bat, cab; B. reads; C. mop, box; D. Check students' tracing. E. Answers will vary.

Week 15, Day 3 (page 75)
A. Fish move their tails side to side. B. Nouns: ship, bread, apple; Verbs: write, clean, throw; C. boat; D. o, s, m, e; Answers will vary. E. Check students' coloring.

Week 15, Day 4 (page 76)
A. I have a blue cup. B. Check students' circling. C. Kelly; D. Answers will vary. E. friend, draw

Week 16, Day 1 (page 77)
A. Answers will vary. B. Across: mitt; Down: sink; C. hose (accept shoe), cone, rope (accept pore); D. ro/bot, ti/ger, pi/lot; E. People and teapots can both shout.

Week 16, Day 2 (page 78)
A. Answers will vary. Letters should make the word *ground*; B. drives; C. hot, dot, pot; D. Check students' tracing. E. Answers will vary but drawings should show order.

Week 16, Day 3 (page 79)
A. boy, coin; B. Check students' drawing. C. horse; D. Answers will vary. E. how, just, any

Week 16, Day 4 (page 80)
A. Answers will vary. B. Check students' spelling. C. Friday; D. Check students' tracing. E. Answers will vary.

Week 17, Day 1 (page 81)
A. character: giant, Jack; setting: beanstalk, castle; B. fish, ocean, reef, wave, whale; C. bumpy, black, quick, nine; D. 2, 1, 2; E. The little boy ran away.

Answer Key

Week 17, Day 2 (page 82)
A. dog, top, fox, cat; B. eat; C. log, fox;
D. Check students' tracing. E. Answers will
vary.

Week 17, Day 3 (page 83)
A. This cookie is for Mommy, but all of those
with sprinkles are for me. B. Nouns: officer,
grandma, boy; Pronouns: she, you, we;
C. tree; D. e, w, r, e; Answers will vary.
E. Check students' coloring.

Week 17, Day 4 (page 84)
A. Two purple monsters ate pizza. B. Check
students' circling. C. March; D. c, p, u;
E. It feels soft. The child had fun and does
not want to leave.

Week 18, Day 1 (page 85)
A. Answers will vary. B. Across: sock;
Down: doll; C. mule, cube, cute; D. o/pen,
si/lent, pa/per; E. Answers will vary but
drawing should show an animal sleeping
in a dwelling.

Week 18, Day 2 (page 86)
A. Answers will vary. Letters should make the
word *watch*. B. nap; C. rug, bug, mug;
D. Check students' tracing. E. Answers will
vary but drawings should show order.

Week 18, Day 3 (page 87)
A. crown, mouse; B. Check students'
drawing. C. purple; D. Answers will vary.
E. from, put, know

Week 18, Day 4 (page 88)
A. Answers will vary. B. Check students'
spelling. C. New York City; D. Check
students' tracing. E. Answers will vary.

Week 19, Day 1 (page 89)
A. character: dwarf, Snow White; setting:
cottage, woods; B. cloud, rain, snow, storm,
wind; C. curvy, heavy, green; D. 2, 1, 2;
E. Check students' coloring to see an
uppercase *U*.

Week 19, Day 2 (page 90)
A. crab, train, bread, flag; B. swim; C. bus,
rug; D. Check students' tracing. E. Answers
will vary.

Week 19, Day 3 (page 91)
A. The Eiffel Tower is in Paris, France.
B. Nouns: shoe, library, peach; Adjectives:
soft, quiet, purple; C. scarf; D. g, i, e,
v; Answers will vary. E. Check students'
coloring.

Week 19, Day 4 (page 92)
A. Ellie went to school today. B. Check
students' circling. C. Alaska; D. t, h, a;
E. They went to the store. They bought rice,
beans, milk, a cookie, and apples.

Week 20, Day 1 (page 93)
A. Answers will vary. B. Across: hand; Down:
flag; C. bird, girl, stir; D. hab/it, hu/man,
pret/zel; E. He should be in bed sleeping.
Explanations will vary.

Week 20, Day 2 (page 94)
A. Answers will vary. Letters should make the
word *apple*. B. shines; C. key, pencil, mug;
D. Check students' tracing. E. Answers will
vary but drawings should show order.

Week 20, Day 3 (page 95)
A. broom, spoon; B. Students should draw a
line through the last sentence. C. bus;
D. Answers will vary. E. take, every, old

Answer Key

Week 20, Day 4 (page 96)
A. Answers will vary. B. Check students' spelling. C. Answers will vary. D. Check students' tracing. E. Answers will vary.

Week 21, Day 1 (page 97)
A. character: Hansel, witch; setting: candy house, woods; B. axle, lever, pulley, wedge, wheel; C. swim, run, yell; D. rac/coon, des/ert, af/ter; E. Answers will vary but could include happy or relaxed. Explanations will vary.

Week 21, Day 2 (page 98)
A. stop, brick, drip, dress; B. will watch; C. bug, sun; D. Check students' tracing. E. Answers will vary.

Week 21, Day 3 (page 99)
A. What did one balloon say to another balloon at the party? B. Adjectives: yellow, spiky, lazy; Verbs: leap, swim, cook; C. girl; D. j, s, u, t; Answers will vary. E. Check students' coloring.

Week 21, Day 4 (page 100)
A. That is my yellow coat. B. Check students' circling. C. Answers will vary. D. p, e, t; E. They brought a map and water. They see birds fly out of the trees and they hear twigs snap.

Week 22, Day 1 (page 101)
A. Answers will vary. B. dress, nest; C. fern, nurse, purse; D. pa/per, quick/ly, bak/er; E. an otter's special parts; how an otter eats

Week 22, Day 2 (page 102)
A. Answers will vary. Letters should make the word *father*. B. will draw; C. skip, talk, hide; D. Check students' tracing. E. Answers will vary.

Week 22, Day 3 (page 103)
A. foot, hook; B. Check students' drawing. C. shark; D. Answers will vary. E. by, after, think

Week 22, Day 4 (page 104)
A. Answers will vary. B. Check students' spelling. C. Answers will vary. D. Check students' tracing. E. Answers will vary.

Week 23, Day 1 (page 105)
A. Henry/he, Mom and I/we, Mrs. Roberts/she, tree/it; B. butterfly, caterpillar, chrysalis, egg, larva; C. walk, shout, toss; D. gui/tar, sum/mer, tea/cher; E. *morning* because it is the only noun or *raining* because it has a different vowel sound

Week 23, Day 2 (page 106)
A. sink, hand, raft, cord; B. kicked; C. cake, vase; D. Check students' tracing. E. Answers will vary.

Week 23, Day 3 (page 107)
A. You can hear blood moving inside your head when you hold a shell to your ear. B. Adjectives: silly, bright, warm; Adverbs: slowly, gently, quickly; C. leaf; D. n, e, o, p; Answers will vary. E. Check students' coloring.

Week 23, Day 4 (page 108)
A. Owls cannot move their eyes side to side. B. Check students' circling. C. Answers will vary. D. o, d, t; E. The baby brother always cries. Answers will vary.

Week 24, Day 1 (page 109)
A. Answers will vary. B. brick, fish; C. chalk, cherry, chick; *ch* circled; D. re/view, un/do, dis/like; E. to go down, Answers will vary.

Answer Key

Week 24, Day 2 (page 110)
A. Answers will vary. Letters should make the word *garden*. B. chased; C. sharp, blue, angry; D. Check students' tracing. E. Answers will vary.

Week 24, Day 3 (page 111)
A. chair, bear; B. something to show how it sounds; to call your attention to the word; C. bird; D. Answers will vary. E. walk, let, going

Week 24, Day 4 (page 112)
A. Answers will vary. B. Check students' spelling. C. Answers will vary. D. Check students' tracing. E. Answers will vary.

Week 25, Day 1 (page 113)
A. house/it, Kayla and I/we, Mr. Lang/he, Lori/she; B. add, equals, number, subtract, symbol; C. leap, exclaim, sleep; D. gar/den, cir/cle, lit/tle; E. Students should underline was, lived, swam, climbed, snapped, and caught.

Week 25, Day 2 (page 114)
A. ship, whale, chin, thorn; B. wrote; C. dice, kite; D. Check students' tracing. E. Answers will vary.

Week 25, Day 3 (page 115)
A. What has four wheels and flies?
B. Prefixes: untie, dislike, mistake; Suffixes: hopeful, careless, happier; C. stool; D. w, o, k, n; Answers will vary. E. Check students' coloring.

Week 25, Day 4 (page 116)
A. How do plants make food? B. Check students' circling. C. Answers will vary. D. p, t, c, u; E. Pam reads two new books. Pam plays a game on the computer.

Week 26, Day 1 (page 117)
A. Answers will vary. B. Across: lock; down: frog; C. shark, shelf, shirt; *sh* circled; D. mis/spell, re/place, un/known; E. Answers will vary but could include a picture of each step and the finished fan.

Week 26, Day 2 (page 118)
A. Answers will vary. Letters should make the word *chicken*. B. ring; C. charlie, texas, july; D. Check students' tracing. E. Answers will vary.

Week 26, Day 3 (page 119)
A. couch, frown; B. Check students' drawing. C. towel; D. Answers will vary. E. again, may, stop

Week 26, Day 4 (page 120)
A. Answers will vary. B. Check students' spelling. C. Answers will vary. D. Check students' tracing. E. Answers will vary.

Week 27, Day 1 (page 121)
A. David's/his, Mom and Dad's/their, Lucy's/her; B. Answers will vary. C. clap, bake, type; D. dis/like, pre/heat, un/lock; E. Answers will vary but could include lazy and sleepy.

Week 27, Day 2 (page 122)
A. match, dish, teeth, wing; B. work; C. rope, cone; D. ch; E. Answers will vary.

Week 27, Day 3 (page 123)
A. The first day of January is called New Year's Day. B. Prefixes: preview, reread, unfair; Suffixes: trying, useless, kindness; C. fly; D. n, e, w, h; Answers will vary. E. Check students' coloring.

Answer Key

Week 27, Day 4 (page 124)
A. The baby dropped her snack and cried.
B. Check students' circling. C. Answers will vary. D. a, t, h, o; E. Answers will vary but could include tasty or delicious. Jake likes Fran because he asks her to help.

Week 28, Day 1 (page 125)
A. Answers will vary. B. Across: drum; Down: brush; C. thank, three, thumb; *th* circled; D. pain/less, dark/ness, peach/es; E. Answers will vary but should include something about eyes.

Week 28, Day 2 (page 126)
A. Answers will vary. Letters should make the word *brother*. B. stalks; C. Paper, Seat, Month; D. sh; E. Answers will vary.

Week 28, Day 3 (page 127)
A. rabbit, butter, balloon; B. Check students' drawing. C. cake; D. Answers will vary. E. give, round, fly

Week 28, Day 4 (page 128)
A. Answers will vary. B. Check students' spelling. C. Answers will vary. D. Check students' tracing. E. Answers will vary.

Week 29, Day 1 (page 129)
A. singular: anyone, everything; plural: both, many; B. Answers will vary. C. build, watch, quit; D. care/ful (or hope/ful), jump/ing, hope/less (or care/less); E. dainty, dear, little, bright, shiny, velvety, pretty, pink, lovely, white, soft, furry; Answers will vary but may include that the author likes the kitten because the author uses positive words to describe the kitten.

Week 29, Day 2 (page 130)
A. boat, mule, gate, dime; B. talk; C. cube, mule; D. th; E. Answers will vary.

Week 29, Day 3 (page 131)
A. Mom put pickles, cheese, and ketchup on Dad's sandwich. B. Happy: joyful, merry, cheerful; Sad: upset, gloomy, blue; C. pie; D. n, o, c, e; Answers will vary. E. Check students' coloring.

Week 29, Day 4 (page 132)
A. The firefighter carries a heavy hose. or, A firefighter carries the heavy hose. B. Check students' circling. C. Answers will vary. D. o, t, n, s; E. Answers will vary.

Week 30, Day 1 (page 133)
A. Answers will vary. B. Across: mouse; Down: clown; C. whale, wheat, whisk; *wh* circled; D. qui/et, sweet/est, short/er; E. Answers will vary.

Week 30, Day 2 (page 134)
A. Answers will vary. Letters should make the word *morning*. B. pulled; C. huge, giant, immense; D. wh; E. Answers will vary.

Week 30, Day 3 (page 135)
A. lamp, truck, pie; B. Check students' drawing. C. pot; D. Answers will vary. E. has, open, live

Week 30, Day 4 (page 136)
A. Answers will vary. B. Check students' spelling. C. Answers will vary. D. Check students' tracing. E. Answers will vary.

Week 31, Day 1 (page 137)
A. singular: each, anything; plural: few, many; B. Answers will vary. C. don't, isn't, won't; D. Answers will vary but could include unhook, hooked, review, or viewing. E. suspected or thought

Answer Key

Week 31, Day 2 (page 138)
A. boot, cart, ball, bow; B. will sing; C. snail, chain; D. ch; E. Answers will vary.

Week 31, Day 3 (page 139)
A. I took Sid's dog for a walk, fed it dinner, and brushed its fur. B. Good: great, wonderful; Bad: awful, lousy; C. bread; D. f, e, t, a; Answers will vary. E. Check students' coloring.

Week 31, Day 4 (page 140)
A. Look at that bird fly fast! B. Check students' circling. C. Answers will vary. D. n, b, b, o, x; E. Answers will vary.

Week 32, Day 1 (page 141)
A. Answers will vary. B. Across: moon; Down: broom; C. king, thing, spring; *ng* circled; D. brave, large, give; E. Answers will vary. Andrew Johnson and Harry Truman

Week 32, Day 2 (page 142)
A. Answers will vary. Letters should make the word *children*. B. picked; C. swift, fast, quick; D. sh; E. Answers will vary.

Week 32, Day 3 (page 143)
A. monkey, cherry, baby; B. Check students' drawing. C. foot; D. Answers will vary. E. give, thank, once

Week 32, Day 4 (page 144)
A. Answers will vary. B. Check students' spelling. C. Answers will vary. D. Check students' tracing. E. Answers will vary.

Week 33, Day 1 (page 145)
A. drives/present, jumped/past, will call/future, laughed/past; B. Answers will vary. C. she'll, I'll, they'll; D. Answers will vary but may include undrinkable and cleaning. E. a cup

Week 33, Day 2 (page 146)
A. cone, owl, mouse, foot; B. travel; C. teeth, peach; D. th; E. Answers will vary.

Week 33, Day 3 (page 147)
A. A cat sniffs at its food carefully to make sure it's fresh. B. Big: huge, large; Little: small, tiny; C. turtle; D. t, a, n, h; Answers will vary. E. Check students' coloring.

Week 33, Day 4 (page 148)
A. I want to eat dessert before dinner. B—C. Answers will vary. D. b, s, d, i, f; E. She is in a spaceship. Words like *flew*, *space*, and *moon* were clues.

Week 34, Day 1 (page 149)
A. Answers will vary. B. Across: gate; Down: snail; C. teeth, beach, leash; D. talk/ing, fast/er, pre/school; E. parts of an apple, flesh and skin

Week 34, Day 2 (page 150)
A. Answers will vary. Letters should make the word *birthday*. B. talk; C. preview, unlike, rewind; D. ck; E. Answers will vary.

Week 34, Day 3 (page 151)
A. teapot, peanut, lightbulb; B. Check students' drawing. C. talk; D. Answers will vary. E. red, yellow, orange

Answer Key

Week 34, Day 4 (page 152)
A. Answers will vary. B. Check students´ spelling. C. Answers will vary. D. Check students´ tracing. E. Answers will vary.

Week 35, Day 1 (page 153)
A. slobbered/past, sleeps/present, will eat/ future, cries/present; B. Answers will vary. C. I´d, he´d, we´d; D. Answers will vary but may include helpful and preread. E. Answers will vary but may include to make the poem fun to read.

Week 35, Day 2 (page 154)
A. square, watch, catch, spring; B. tie, C. toast, throw; D. ng; E. Answers will vary.

Week 35, Day 3 (page 155)
A. Why did the golfer wear two pairs of pants? B. Walk: march, stroll; Look: glance, watch; C. cloud; D. e, e, v, r; Answers will vary. D. Check students' coloring.

Week 35, Day 4 (page 156)
A. The angry child stomped up the stairs. B—C. Answers will vary. D. b, t, o, g; E. Answers will vary but may include that Deer ate the carrots; generous

Week 36, Day 1 (page 157)
A. Answers will vary. B. Across: peach; Down: cheese; C. paint, spray, steak (or stake); D. re/view, turn/ing, small/est; E. chicken life cycle, Answers will vary.

Week 36, Day 2 (page 158)
A. Answers will vary. Letters should make the word *picture*. B. rotates; C. fearless, baker, careful; D. qu; E. Answers will vary.

Week 36, Day 3 (page 159)
A. pumpkin, robot, tiger; B. plants, alphabetical; C. robe; D. Answers will vary. E. purple, blue, green

Week 36, Day 4 (page 160)
A. Answers will vary. B. Check students´ spelling. C. Answers will vary. D. Check students´ tracing. E. Answers will vary.

Week 37, Day 1 (page 161)
A. will jump/future, stare/present, will write/future, chased/past; B. Answers will vary. C. she´s, they´ve, you´ve; D. Answers will vary but may include preheat and reacting. E. It is still light out and people are still outside.

Week 37, Day 2 (page 162)
A. cane, tube, tape, kite; B. will decide; C. chair, shark; D. ph; E. Answers will vary.

Week 37, Day 3 (page 163)
A. A tornado can strip bark from trees and pluck feathers from a chicken. B. Laugh: giggle, chuckle; Said: shout, exclaim; C. camel; D. i, a, a, g; Answers will vary. E. Check students´ coloring.

Week 37, Day 4 (page 164)
A. When do I go to my piano lesson? B—C. Answers will vary. D. l, p, r, d, i, t; E. The students need to wear a yellow shirt and bring lunch and a drink; excited

Week 38, Day 1 (page 165)
A. Answers will vary. B. Across: fries; Down: knight; C. small, crawl, sauce; D. friend/ly, wrong/ly, kind/ness; E. travels

Answer Key

Week 38, Day 2 (page 166)
A. Answers will vary. Letters should make the word *Thanksgiving*. B. will wash; C. likely, unlike, likeness; D. kn; E. Answers will vary.

Week 38, Day 3 (page 167)
A. tree, cow, house; B. Check students' drawing. C. scratchy; D. Answers will vary but should include text about fruit or fruit trees. E. black, brown, gray

Week 38, Day 4 (page 168)
A. Answers will vary. B. Check students' spelling. C. Answers will vary. D. Check students' tracing. E. Answers will vary.

Week 39, Day 1 (page 169)
A. blinks/present, shouted/past, gobbles/present, will ask/future; B. Answers will vary. C. she's, I'm, we're; D. Answers will vary but may include joyful and fearless. E. Answers will vary but should include something about the life cycle of a butterfly.

Week 39, Day 2 (page 170)
A. paws, claw, coin, news; B. punted; C. mouse, screw; D. tch; E. Answers will vary.

Week 39, Day 3 (page 171)
A. What is at the end of everything? B. Eat: gobble, feast; Sleep: nap, doze; C. knife; D. u, c, o, l; Answers will vary. E. Check students' coloring.

Week 39, Day 4 (page 172)
A. I want to go to the park, but it is raining. B—C. Answers will vary. D. i, s, t, a; E. Answers will vary.

Week 40, Day 1 (page 173)
A. Answers will vary. B. throne, coach; C. crown, towel, bounce; D. box/es, re/do, high/er; E. It means that you do not have to add that ingredient.

Week 40, Day 2 (page 174)
A. Answers will vary. Letters should make the word *toothbrush*. B. types; C. replay, playing, playful; D. dge; E. Answers will vary.

Week 40, Day 3 (page 175)
A. basket, snowman, pencil; B. Check students' drawing. C. slow; D. Answers will vary. E. white, pink, violet

Week 40, Day 4 (page 176)
A. Answers will vary. B. Check students' spelling. C. Answers will vary. D. Check students' tracing. Answers will vary.